Contents

Essential Background Information

The 10 Powerful Steps of the Magic Sequence

Resources

Why does multiplication fluency matter?

Multiplication fluency unlocks a wide spectrum of skills ranging from fractions and proportions to exponents and equations. In turn, these concepts are needed to more easily unlock the algebra doorway.

This is why students should memorize their multiplication facts by heart as quickly as possible.

When students have multiplication fluency and when their fact recall is automated, it unlocks doors, and it allows them to focus their mental energy on problem solving.

How does this system help?

This system can help build multiplication fluency **faster and more easily than has been possible in the past.** It works because it was designed based on how the brain learns, and it's easier to use than the standard times table and the random drills that often come with it.

As a result, rather than being frustrated for months or even years, students can learn their multiplication facts by heart in about a month in the third grade, giving them the confidence they need to take learning to a higher level.

Think of sea turtles. While on land, sea turtles travel slowly and need a great deal of effort to get from place to place. However, once in the water, sea turtles are actually very strong swimmers, and they can navigate the ocean freely. Sea turtles are confident and feel at home in the ocean because they are fluent swimmers.

The same thing happens with multiplication fluency.

Once students gain multiplication fluency, they can navigate an ocean of math concepts much more freely. Concepts from fractions and proportions to exponents and equations become much easier to understand, and students feel at home with math. Multiplication fluency gives students the confidence and the tools that they need to take learning to a higher level. This system helps build that fluency.

The Core Advantage math fluency system was developed by Dr. Randy Palisoc, a Co-Founder of the five-time national award-winning Synergy Academies. In 2013, the National Center for Urban School Transformation named Synergy's elementary school the #1 Urban Elementary School in America. Dr. Palisoc has also been featured as a TEDx speaker. His TEDx talk can be found by googling "**randy palisoc ted talk**."

CORE ADVANTAGE®

10 Powerful Steps to
Multiplication
FLUENCY

DR. RANDY PALISOC

IRONBOX®
Education

IRONBOX®
Education

The Magic Sequence

*These are the 10 Powerful Steps to Multiplication Fluency. Visit **MathFluency.com** to see the demo video.*

Step One

2
Twos

2 x 1 = **2**
2 x 2 = **4**
2 x 3 = **6**
2 x 4 = **8**
2 x 5 = **10**
2 x 6 = **12**
2 x 7 = **14**
2 x 8 = **16**
2 x 9 = **18**

Step Two

3
Threes

3 x 1 = **3**
3 x 2 = **6**
3 x 3 = **9**
3 x 4 = **12**
3 x 5 = **15**
3 x 6 = **18**
3 x 7 = **21**
3 x 8 = **24**
3 x 9 = **27**

Step Three

4
Fours

4 x 1 = **4**
4 x 2 = **8**
4 x 3 = **12**
4 x 4 = **16**
4 x 5 = **20**
4 x 6 = **24**
4 x 7 = **28**
4 x 8 = **32**
4 x 9 = **36**

Step Four

5
Fives

5 x 1 = **5**
5 x 2 = **10**
5 x 3 = **15**
5 x 4 = **20**
5 x 5 = **25**
5 x 6 = **30**
5 x 7 = **35**
5 x 8 = **40**
5 x 9 = **45**

Step Five

9
Nines

9 x 1 = **9**
9 x 2 = **18**
9 x 3 = **27**
9 x 4 = **36**
9 x 5 = **45**
9 x 6 = **54**
9 x 7 = **63**
9 x 8 = **72**
9 x 9 = **81**

Magic Box

Step Six

Squares

1 x 1 = **1**
2 x 2 = **4**
3 x 3 = **9**
4 x 4 = **16**
5 x 5 = **25**
6 x 6 = **36**
7 x 7 = **49**
8 x 8 = **64**
9 x 9 = **81**

Step Seven

Big Bad Numbers

6 x 6 = **36**   7 x 7 = **49**   8 x 8 = **64**   9 x 9 = **81**
6 x 7 = **42**   7 x 8 = **56**   8 x 9 = **72**
6 x 8 = **48**   7 x 9 = **63**
6 x 9 = **54**

Magic Triangle

Step Eight

6
Sixes

6 x 1 = **6**
6 x 2 = **12**
6 x 3 = **18**
6 x 4 = **24**
6 x 5 = **30**
6 x 6 = **36**
6 x 7 = **42**
6 x 8 = **48**
6 x 9 = **54**

Step Nine

7
Sevens

7 x 1 = **7**
7 x 2 = **14**
7 x 3 = **21**
7 x 4 = **28**
7 x 5 = **35**
7 x 6 = **42**
7 x 7 = **49**
7 x 8 = **56**
7 x 9 = **63**

Step Ten

8
Eights

8 x 1 = **8**
8 x 2 = **16**
8 x 3 = **24**
8 x 4 = **32**
8 x 5 = **40**
8 x 6 = **48**
8 x 7 = **56**
8 x 8 = **64**
8 x 9 = **72**

How to Use This Multiplication Fluency System

Before using this multiplication fluency system with students, ***please be sure to watch demo videos #1-10 online first.*** The demo videos explain in more detail how the different components work.

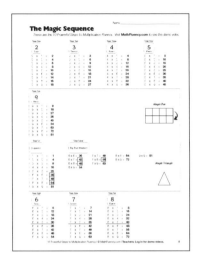

The Magic Sequence

This is the Magic Sequence, and these are the 10 Powerful Steps to Multiplication Fluency:

Step One	Step Two	Step Three	Step Four	Step Five	Step Six	Step Seven	Step Eight	Step Nine	Step Ten
2 Twos	**3** Threes	**4** Fours	**5** Fives	**9** Nines	Squares	Big Bad Numbers	**6** Sixes	**7** Sevens	**8** Eights

The Magic Sequence is easier to learn than the traditional times table. The activities in this system help students memorize the multiplication facts that are presented in the Magic Sequence.

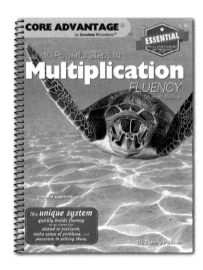

Coil-Bound Student Edition
(folds back upon itself and lays flat)

Students work out of a coil-bound student edition, which folds back upon itself and lays flat (this is necessary because of the flipping and folding of pages that are part of the system). The coil-bound student edition contains the following student materials:

- A copy of the Magic Sequence
- Practice Pages for Steps 1-10 (for building fluency)
- Perforated Study Cards
- Appendix A and Appendix B (for building conceptual understanding)

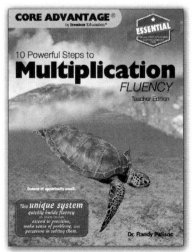

Teacher Edition

In addition to blank copies of the Practice Pages as well as Appendix A and Appendix B (all included in the coil-bound student edition), the teacher edition contains the following:

- Handwritten answer keys
- Blank copy of Appendix C (extra Memory Builders for use when using a two-day pacing plan)

Practice Pages (in coil-bound student edition)

The coil-bound student edition contains ten sets of Practice Pages (one set for each step of the Magic Sequence). The cover page for Step One (The Twos) is shown to the left. Each set of Practice Pages contains the following essential activities:

- Speed Builders #1-4
- Memory Builder
- Distributed Practice (homework)

Speed Builders #1-4   Memory Builder   Distributed Practice
(super important, see video)

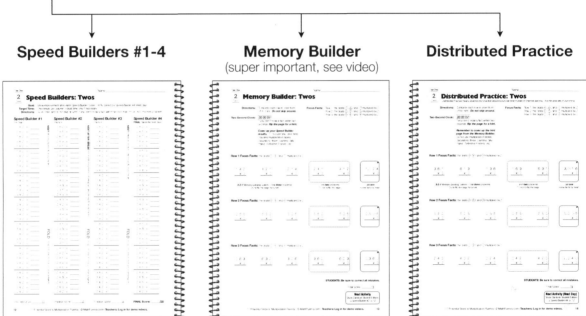

Please watch the demo videos online for detailed explanations of how each activity works.

Study Cards (in coil-bound student edition)

The coil-bound student edition also contains perforated Study Cards that accompany the activities in the Practice Pages.

Use the Study Cards in preparation for Speed Builders #2, #3, and #4.

Do not use the Study Cards before Speed Builder #1, which is a pre-test that should be taken cold.

On the next page, the Action Plan and Success Tracker will explain when to use the Speed Builders, Memory Builders, Distributed Practice, and Study Cards.

Action Plan and Success Tracker

Notice that the cover page of each set of Practice Pages has an Action Plan and Success Tracker in the bottom right corner, as shown here.

Students complete each activity (Speed Builders, Memory Builders, Distributed Practice and Study Cards) in the order shown on this checklist. See Pacing Options #1 and #2 below.

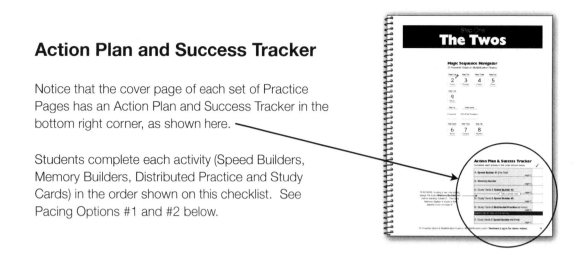

Pacing Option #1 (One day per set of Practice Pages, 11 consecutive days total)

Action Plan & Success Tracker
Complete each activity in the order shown below. ✓

Complete on the same day. ⎰

A. **Speed Builder #1** (Pre-Test)
page 12

B. **Memory Builder**
page 13

C. Study Cards & **Speed Builder #2**
Take a break now.
page 12

D. Study Cards & **Speed Builder #3**
page 12

E. Study Cards & **Distributed Practice** (at home)
page 15

Speed Builder #4: Wait until the next day.

Wait until the next day. ⎰

F. Study Cards & **Speed Builder #4** (Final)
page 12

Pacing Option #2 (Two days per set of Practice Pages, 21 consecutive days total)

Use this two-day pacing if students need additional practice and support. The Memory Builder is an especially important activity, so **assign an extra Memory Builder** before Activity D on the second day of each set of Practice Pages, as shown below. The extra Memory Builders are found in **Appendix C of the Teacher Edition,** starting on page 79.

Action Plan & Success Tracker
Complete each activity in the order shown below. ✓

Day 1 ⎰

A. **Speed Builder #1** (Pre-Test)
page 12

B. **Memory Builder**
page 13

C. Study Cards & **Speed Builder #2**
Take a break now.
page 12

Assign an Extra **Memory Builder** here. ➤

Day 2 ⎰

D. Study Cards & **Speed Builder #3**
page 12

E. Study Cards & **Distributed Practice** (at home)
page 15

Speed Builder #4: Wait until the next day.

Wait until the next day. ⎰

F. Study Cards & **Speed Builder #4** (Final)
page 12

Appendix A and Appendix B (in Student Edition)

The Ten Steps of the Magic Sequence are designed to build multiplication fluency. Appendix A and Appendix B are bookends that complement the system, and they are designed to build conceptual understanding.

- Use Appendix A **before** using Step One.
- Use Appendix B only **after** completing Step Ten.

Appendix C (page 79 in Teacher Edition)

Appendix C contains the **Extra "Memory Builders"** that should be assigned to students when using the two-day pacing option shown on the previous page. Assign the Extra "Memory Builder" before Activity D (Study Cards and Speed Builder #3) on the second day of each Practice Booklet.

The Extra "Memory Builders" may also be used as refresher lessons. For example, after students have completed Steps 1-10, the teacher may review Steps 1-10 by assigning an Extra "Memory Builder" each day for ten days.

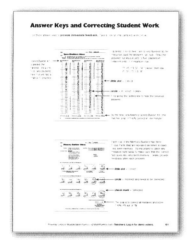

Answer Keys (page 101 in Teacher Edition)

All answer keys are handwritten and fully-annotated. Please be sure to provide immediate feedback to students.

Page 101 describes the **specific correction marks and procedures** that should be used for the following activities:

- Speed Builders
- Memory Builders & Distributed Practice

Pretests/Posttests (page 114 in Teacher Edition)

There are two pretests/posttests that teachers may use:

- Single-digit Pretest/Posttest (100 problems, four minutes)
- Multi-digit by Single-digit Pretest/Posttest (20 problems, seven minutes)

Administer both pretests before students start using the multiplication fluency system. Administer both posttests after students have completed the system.

Addressing State Learning Standards or the Common Core State Standards

Today, schools across America are either using their own state's learning standards or the Common Core State Standards.

No matter what learning standards a school is using, this system helps give students an academic advantage by building fluency faster than has been possible in the past. Fluency is important for all students because it helps them be more precise, which in turn helps them more easily make sense of math.

Take a look at these two Standards for Mathematical Practice (MP), which are used by states using the Common Core State Standards:

> MP #1: Make sense of problems and persevere in solving them.
> MP #6: Attend to precision.

How do these two math practices go together?

- If students **cannot** attend to precision (#6), then they will not make sense of problems (#1), and they will not persevere in solving them (#1).

On the other hand,

- If students **can** attend to precision (#6), then they are more likely to make sense of problems (#1) and are more likely to persevere in solving them (#1).

As you can see, attending to precision (#6) can mean the difference between confidence and confusion.

The unique Core Advantage system used in this book can help give students an academic advantage in a short amount of time. It is designed to build fluency so that students can attend to precision (#6) and actually understand what they're doing in math.

It does take hard work and practice on the part of students, and only students themselves can determine their level of success based on their effort. The good news is that the greater their level of fluency, the more confidence students will have, and the more likely they are to persevere and put in that necessary hard work and practice.

Fluency matters, and I hope that you are able to use this system to build that fluency with your students.

-- Dr. Randy Palisoc

The Twos

Magic Sequence Navigator

10 Powerful Steps to Multiplication Fluency

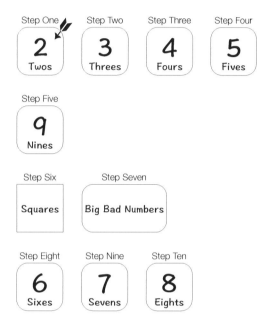

Step One	Step Two	Step Three	Step Four
2 Twos	**3** Threes	**4** Fours	**5** Fives

Step Five
9 Nines

Step Six	Step Seven
Squares	Big Bad Numbers

Step Eight	Step Nine	Step Ten
6 Sixes	**7** Sevens	**8** Eights

Action Plan & Success Tracker

Complete each activity in the order shown below.   ✓

REMINDER: Before starting Step One, use the guided lessons in Appendix A-1, A-2, A-3, and A-4 in order to build conceptual understanding of multiplication. page 71	
A. **Speed Builder #1** (Pre-Test) page 12	
B. **Memory Builder** page 13	
C. Study Cards & **Speed Builder #2** Take a break now. page 12	
D. Study Cards & **Speed Builder #3** page 12	
E. Study Cards & **Distributed Practice** (at home) page 15	
Speed Builder #4: Wait until the next day.	
F. Study Cards & **Speed Builder #4** (Final) page 12	

TEACHERS: If using a two-day pacing, assign the Extra **Memory Builder** here, before starting Activity D. The Extra Memory Builder is found in the teacher edition on page 81.

Step One

2 Twos

Speed Builders: Twos

Name_____

Goal: Show improvement after each Speed Builder. Score 100% correct by Speed Builder #4 (next day).
Target Time: One minute per column. Adjust time only if necessary.
Directions: Go in order, and do not skip around. If you don't recall a fact within two seconds, move on to the next problem.

Speed Builder #1 Pre-Test	Speed Builder #2 Practice	Speed Builder #3 Practice	Speed Builder #4 FINAL (taken the next day)
2 x 2 = ___	2 x 2 = ___	2 x 2 = ___	2 x 2 = ___
5 x 2 = ___	2 x 5 = ___	5 x 2 = ___	2 x 5 = ___
7 x 2 = ___	2 x 7 = ___	7 x 2 = ___	2 x 7 = ___
9 x 2 = ___	2 x 9 = ___	9 x 2 = ___	2 x 9 = ___
6 x 2 = ___	2 x 6 = ___	6 x 2 = ___	2 x 6 = ___
5 x 2 = ___	2 x 5 = ___	5 x 2 = ___	2 x 5 = ___
9 x 2 = ___	2 x 9 = ___	9 x 2 = ___	2 x 9 = ___
2 x 2 = ___	2 x 2 = ___	2 x 2 = ___	2 x 2 = ___
7 x 2 = ___	2 x 7 = ___	7 x 2 = ___	2 x 7 = ___
4 x 2 = ___	2 x 4 = ___	4 x 2 = ___	2 x 4 = ___
6 x 2 = ___	2 x 6 = ___	6 x 2 = ___	2 x 6 = ___
3 x 2 = ___	2 x 3 = ___	3 x 2 = ___	2 x 3 = ___
8 x 2 = ___	2 x 8 = ___	8 x 2 = ___	2 x 8 = ___
5 x 2 = ___	2 x 5 = ___	5 x 2 = ___	2 x 5 = ___
9 x 2 = ___	2 x 9 = ___	9 x 2 = ___	2 x 9 = ___
3 x 2 = ___	2 x 3 = ___	3 x 2 = ___	2 x 3 = ___
2 x 2 = ___	2 x 2 = ___	2 x 2 = ___	2 x 2 = ___
8 x 2 = ___	2 x 8 = ___	8 x 2 = ___	2 x 8 = ___
4 x 2 = ___	2 x 4 = ___	4 x 2 = ___	2 x 4 = ___
7 x 2 = ___	2 x 7 = ___	7 x 2 = ___	2 x 7 = ___
6 x 2 = ___	2 x 6 = ___	6 x 2 = ___	2 x 6 = ___
8 x 2 = ___	2 x 8 = ___	8 x 2 = ___	2 x 8 = ___
3 x 2 = ___	2 x 3 = ___	3 x 2 = ___	2 x 3 = ___
4 x 2 = ___	2 x 4 = ___	4 x 2 = ___	2 x 4 = ___
7 x 2 = ___	2 x 7 = ___	7 x 2 = ___	2 x 7 = ___
3 x 2 = ___	2 x 3 = ___	3 x 2 = ___	2 x 3 = ___
2 x 2 = ___	2 x 2 = ___	2 x 2 = ___	2 x 2 = ___
5 x 2 = ___	2 x 5 = ___	5 x 2 = ___	2 x 5 = ___
4 x 2 = ___	2 x 4 = ___	4 x 2 = ___	2 x 4 = ___
6 x 2 = ___	2 x 6 = ___	6 x 2 = ___	2 x 6 = ___
9 x 2 = ___	2 x 9 = ___	9 x 2 = ___	2 x 9 = ___
8 x 2 = ___	2 x 8 = ___	8 x 2 = ___	2 x 8 = ___
6 x 2 = ___	2 x 6 = ___	6 x 2 = ___	2 x 6 = ___
3 x 2 = ___	2 x 3 = ___	3 x 2 = ___	2 x 3 = ___
2 x 2 = ___	2 x 2 = ___	2 x 2 = ___	2 x 2 = ___

NEXT: Memory Builder & Study Cards

NEXT AFTER (BREAK): Extra Memory Builder (if using two-day pacing) & Study Cards

NEXT: Distributed Practice (at home) & Study Cards

FOLD along dotted line to hide previous answers.

Pre-Test Score:_____ /35   Practice Score: _____ /35   Practice Score: _____ /35   **FINAL Score:** _____ **/35**

2 Twos

Memory Builder: Twos

Name_____

Directions: Complete each row in order from left to right. **Do not skip around.**

Two-Second Clock: `00:00:02`
If you don't recall a fact within two seconds, **flip the page for a hint.**

Cover up your Speed Builder results. Do not use any other hints, including multiplication tables, calculators, finger counting, tally marks, Refresher Posters, etc.

Focus Facts: Row 1: the digits ①, ④, and ⑦ multiplied by 2
Row 2: the digits ②, ⑤, and ⑧ multiplied by 2
Row 3: the digits ③, ⑥, and ⑨ multiplied by 2

Row 1 Focus Facts: the digits ①, ④, and ⑦ multiplied by 2

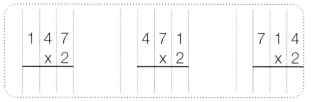

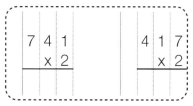

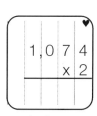

3-2-1 Memory Building System – First **three** problems: OK to flip the page for a hint.

Next **two** problems: Try not to flip the page.

Last **one:** Know facts by heart.

Row 2 Focus Facts: the digits ②, ⑤, and ⑧ multiplied by 2

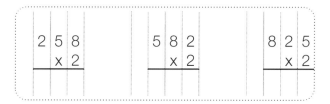

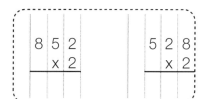

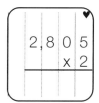

Row 3 Focus Facts: the digits ③, ⑥, and ⑨ multiplied by 2

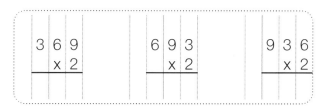

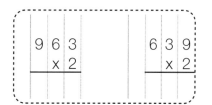

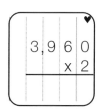

STUDENTS: Be sure to correct all mistakes.

Final Score: _____/18

Next Activity
Study Cards (in Student Edition)
& Speed Builder #2, p. 12

Step One

2

Twos

**Here's
your hint.**

Multiples
of two

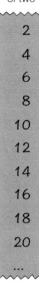

2

4

6

8

10

12

14

16

18

20

...

Make sure this page is hidden/covered and not easily seen when working on the *Memory Builders* and *Distributed Practice.*

With your pencil, touch the multiples of two in the correct order from top to bottom while saying,

"One time,"
"two times,"
"three times,"

and so on until you reach the multiple that you're looking for.

Memorize it, flip the page over, and continue working.

Do not write any other hints on this page.

As you rehearse, the facts will move from your short-term memory into your long-term memory.

2
Twos

Distributed Practice: Twos

Name_____

Distributed Practice means spacing your practice sessions out over time in order to improve learning. It is the opposite of cramming.

Directions: Complete each row in order from left to right. *Do not skip around.*

Focus Facts: Row 1: the digits ⑨, ⑥, and ① multiplied by 2
Row 2: the digits ⑧, ⑤, and ③ multiplied by 2
Row 3: the digits ⑦, ④, and ② multiplied by 2

Two-Second Clock: `00:00:02`
If you don't recall a fact within two seconds, **flip the page for a hint.**

Remember to cover up the hint page from the Memory Builder.
Do not use multiplication tables, calculators, finger counting, tally marks, Refresher Posters, etc.

Row 1 Focus Facts: the digits ⑨, ⑥, and ① multiplied by 2

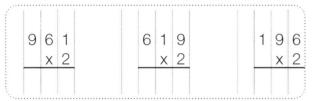

3-2-1 Memory Building System – First *three* problems: OK to flip the page for a hint.

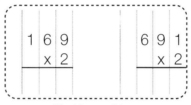

Next *two* problems: Try not to flip the page.

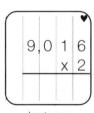

Last *one:* Know facts by heart.

Row 2 Focus Facts: the digits ⑧, ⑤, and ③ multiplied by 2

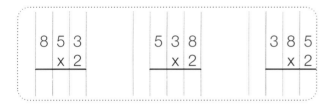

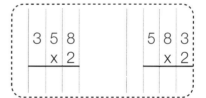

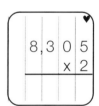

Row 3 Focus Facts: the digits ⑦, ④, and ② multiplied by 2

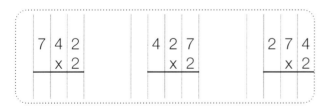

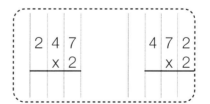

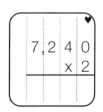

STUDENTS: Be sure to correct all mistakes.

Final Score: _____/18

Next Activity (Next Day)
Study Cards (in Student Edition) & Speed Builder #4, p. 12

Here's your hint.

Multiples of two

| 2 |
| 4 |
| 6 |
| 8 |
| 10 |
| 12 |
| 14 |
| 16 |
| 18 |
| 20 |
| ... |

Make sure this page is hidden/covered and not easily seen when working on the *Memory Builders* and *Distributed Practice.*

With your pencil, touch the multiples of two in the correct order from top to bottom while saying,

"One time,"
"two times,"
"three times,"

and so on until you reach the multiple that you're looking for.

Memorize it, flip the page over, and continue working.

Do not write any other hints on this page.

As you rehearse, the facts will move from your short-term memory into your long-term memory.

Reveal the Pattern: Twos

The multiples of two have created a secret hidden pattern in the Hundred Chart below. Reveal the pattern by *counting by two* and shading in the correct boxes. The first few have been done for you.

1	2	3	4	5	6	7	8	9	10
11	12	13	14	15	16	17	18	19	20
21	22	23	24	25	26	27	28	29	30
31	32	33	34	35	36	37	38	39	40
41	42	43	44	45	46	47	48	49	50
51	52	53	54	55	56	57	58	59	60
61	62	63	64	65	66	67	68	69	70
71	72	73	74	75	76	77	78	79	80
81	82	83	84	85	86	87	88	89	90
91	92	93	94	95	96	97	98	99	100

Step Two
The Threes

Magic Sequence Navigator
10 Powerful Steps to Multiplication Fluency

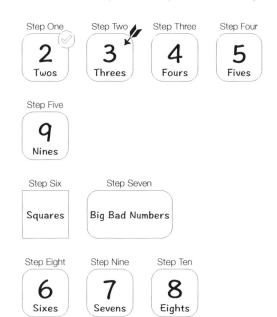

Action Plan & Success Tracker
Complete each activity in the order shown below. ✓

A. **Speed Builder #1** (Pre-Test) page 18	
B. **Memory Builder** page 19	
C. Study Cards & **Speed Builder #2** *Take a break now.* page 18	
D. Study Cards & **Speed Builder #3** page 18	
E. Study Cards & **Distributed Practice** (at home) page 21	
Speed Builder #4: Wait until the next day.	
F. Study Cards & **Speed Builder #4** (Final) page 18	

TEACHERS: If using a two-day pacing, assign the Extra **Memory Builder** here, before starting Activity D. The Extra Memory Builder is found in the teacher edition on page 83.

3 Threes

Speed Builders: Threes

Name_____

Goal: Show improvement after each Speed Builder. Score 100% correct by Speed Builder #4 (next day).
Target Time: One minute per column. Adjust time only if necessary.
Directions: Go in order, and do not skip around. If you don't recall a fact within two seconds, move on to the next problem.

Speed Builder #1
Pre-Test

2 x 3 = _____
5 x 3 = _____
7 x 3 = _____
9 x 3 = _____
6 x 3 = _____

5 x 3 = _____
9 x 3 = _____
2 x 3 = _____
7 x 3 = _____
4 x 3 = _____

6 x 3 = _____
3 x 3 = _____
8 x 3 = _____
5 x 3 = _____
9 x 3 = _____

3 x 3 = _____
2 x 3 = _____
8 x 3 = _____
4 x 3 = _____
7 x 3 = _____

6 x 3 = _____
8 x 3 = _____
3 x 3 = _____
4 x 3 = _____
7 x 3 = _____

3 x 3 = _____
2 x 3 = _____
5 x 3 = _____
4 x 3 = _____
6 x 3 = _____

9 x 3 = _____
8 x 3 = _____
6 x 3 = _____
3 x 3 = _____
2 x 3 = _____

Pre-Test Score:_____/35

NEXT: Memory Builder & Study Cards
FOLD along dotted line to hide previous answers.

Speed Builder #2
Practice

3 x 2 = _____
3 x 5 = _____
3 x 7 = _____
3 x 9 = _____
3 x 6 = _____

3 x 5 = _____
3 x 9 = _____
3 x 2 = _____
3 x 7 = _____
3 x 4 = _____

3 x 6 = _____
3 x 3 = _____
3 x 8 = _____
3 x 5 = _____
3 x 9 = _____

3 x 3 = _____
3 x 2 = _____
3 x 8 = _____
3 x 4 = _____
3 x 7 = _____

3 x 6 = _____
3 x 8 = _____
3 x 3 = _____
3 x 4 = _____
3 x 7 = _____

3 x 3 = _____
3 x 2 = _____
3 x 5 = _____
3 x 4 = _____
3 x 6 = _____

3 x 9 = _____
3 x 8 = _____
3 x 6 = _____
3 x 3 = _____
3 x 2 = _____

Practice Score: _____/35

NEXT AFTER (BREAK): Extra Memory Builder (if using two-day pacing) & Study Cards
FOLD along dotted line to hide previous answers.

Speed Builder #3
Practice

2 x 3 = _____
5 x 3 = _____
7 x 3 = _____
9 x 3 = _____
6 x 3 = _____

5 x 3 = _____
9 x 3 = _____
2 x 3 = _____
7 x 3 = _____
4 x 3 = _____

6 x 3 = _____
3 x 3 = _____
8 x 3 = _____
5 x 3 = _____
9 x 3 = _____

3 x 3 = _____
2 x 3 = _____
8 x 3 = _____
4 x 3 = _____
7 x 3 = _____

6 x 3 = _____
8 x 3 = _____
3 x 3 = _____
4 x 3 = _____
7 x 3 = _____

3 x 3 = _____
2 x 3 = _____
5 x 3 = _____
4 x 3 = _____
6 x 3 = _____

9 x 3 = _____
8 x 3 = _____
6 x 3 = _____
3 x 3 = _____
2 x 3 = _____

Practice Score: _____/35

NEXT: Distributed Practice (at home) & Study Cards
FOLD along dotted line to hide previous answers.

Speed Builder #4
FINAL (taken the next day)

3 x 2 = _____
3 x 5 = _____
3 x 7 = _____
3 x 9 = _____
3 x 6 = _____

3 x 5 = _____
3 x 9 = _____
3 x 2 = _____
3 x 7 = _____
3 x 4 = _____

3 x 6 = _____
3 x 3 = _____
3 x 8 = _____
3 x 5 = _____
3 x 9 = _____

3 x 3 = _____
3 x 2 = _____
3 x 8 = _____
3 x 4 = _____
3 x 7 = _____

3 x 6 = _____
3 x 8 = _____
3 x 3 = _____
3 x 4 = _____
3 x 7 = _____

3 x 3 = _____
3 x 2 = _____
3 x 5 = _____
3 x 4 = _____
3 x 6 = _____

3 x 9 = _____
3 x 8 = _____
3 x 6 = _____
3 x 3 = _____
3 x 2 = _____

FINAL Score: _____/35

10 Powerful Steps to Multiplication Fluency | © MathFluency.com | **Teachers: Log in for demo videos.**

Memory Builder: Threes

Name_____

Directions: Complete each row in order from left to right. **Do not skip around.**

Two-Second Clock: `00:00:02`
If you don't recall a fact within two seconds, **flip the page for a hint.**

Cover up your Speed Builder results. Do not use any other hints, including multiplication tables, calculators, finger counting, tally marks, Refresher Posters, etc.

Focus Facts: Row 1: the digits ①, ④, and ⑦ multiplied by 3
Row 2: the digits ②, ⑤, and ⑧ multiplied by 3
Row 3: the digits ③, ⑥, and ⑨ multiplied by 3

Row 1 Focus Facts: the digits ①, ④, and ⑦ multiplied by 3

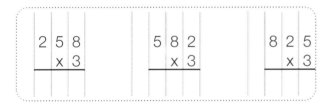
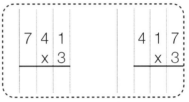
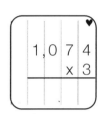

3-2-1 Memory Building System – First **three** problems: OK to flip the page for a hint.

Next **two** problems: Try not to flip the page.

Last **one:** Know facts by heart.

Row 2 Focus Facts: the digits ②, ⑤, and ⑧ multiplied by 3

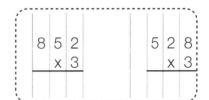
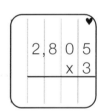

Row 3 Focus Facts: the digits ③, ⑥, and ⑨ multiplied by 3

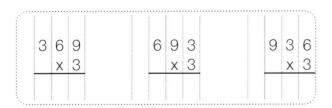
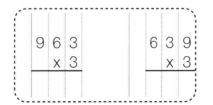
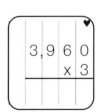

STUDENTS: Be sure to correct all mistakes.

Final Score: _____ /18

Next Activity
Study Cards (in Student Edition) & Speed Builder #2, p. 18

Threes

**Here's
your hint.**

Multiples
of three

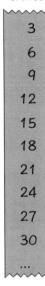

3
6
9
12
15
18
21
24
27
30
...

Make sure this page is hidden/covered and not easily seen when working on the *Memory Builders* and *Distributed Practice.*

With your pencil, touch the multiples of three in the correct order from top to bottom while saying,

> *"One time,"*
> *"two times,"*
> *"three times,"*

and so on until you reach the multiple that you're looking for.

Memorize it, flip the page over, and continue working.

Do not write any other hints on this page.

As you rehearse, the facts will move from your short-term memory into your long-term memory.

Distributed Practice: Threes

Distributed Practice means spacing your practice sessions out over time in order to improve learning. It is the opposite of cramming.

Directions: Complete each row in order from left to right. **Do not skip around.**

Two-Second Clock: `00:00:02`
If you don't recall a fact within two seconds, **flip the page for a hint.**

Remember to cover up the hint page from the Memory Builder. Do not use multiplication tables, calculators, finger counting, tally marks, Refresher Posters, etc.

Focus Facts: Row 1: the digits (9), (6), and (1) multiplied by 3
Row 2: the digits (8), (5), and (3) multiplied by 3
Row 3: the digits (7), (4), and (2) multiplied by 3

Row 1 Focus Facts: the digits (9), (6), and (1) multiplied by 3

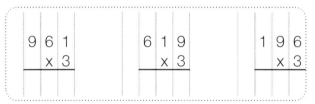

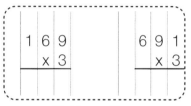

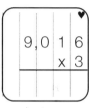

3-2-1 Memory Building System – First **three** problems:
OK to flip the page for a hint.

Next **two** problems:
Try not to flip the page.

Last **one:**
Know facts by heart.

Row 2 Focus Facts: the digits (8), (5), and (3) multiplied by 3

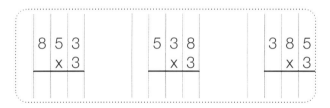

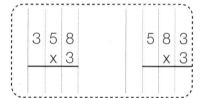

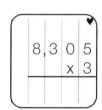

Row 3 Focus Facts: the digits (7), (4), and (2) multiplied by 3

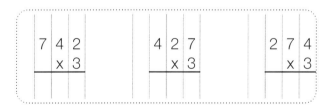

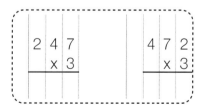

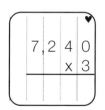

STUDENTS: Be sure to correct all mistakes.

Final Score: _____/18

Next Activity (Next Day)
Study Cards (in Student Edition)
& Speed Builder #4, p. 18

3
6
9
12
15
18
21
24
27
30
...

Make sure this page is hidden/covered and not easily seen when working on the *Memory Builders* and *Distributed Practice.*

With your pencil, touch the multiples of three in the correct order from top to bottom while saying,

"One time,"
"two times,"
"three times,"

and so on until you reach the multiple that you're looking for.

Memorize it, flip the page over, and continue working.

Do not write any other hints on this page.

As you rehearse, the facts will move from your short-term memory into your long-term memory.

Reveal the Pattern: Threes

The multiples of three have created a secret hidden pattern in the Hundred Chart below. Reveal the pattern by **counting by three** and shading in the correct boxes. The first two have been done for you.

1	2	3	4	5	6	7	8	9	10
11	12	13	14	15	16	17	18	19	20
21	22	23	24	25	26	27	28	29	30
31	32	33	34	35	36	37	38	39	40
41	42	43	44	45	46	47	48	49	50
51	52	53	54	55	56	57	58	59	60
61	62	63	64	65	66	67	68	69	70
71	72	73	74	75	76	77	78	79	80
81	82	83	84	85	86	87	88	89	90
91	92	93	94	95	96	97	98	99	100

Magic Sequence Navigator

10 Powerful Steps to Multiplication Fluency

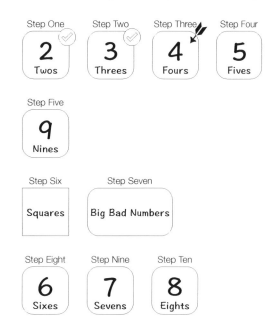

Step One	Step Two	Step Three	Step Four
2 Twos ✓	**3** Threes ✓	**4** Fours	**5** Fives

Step Five
9 Nines

Step Six	Step Seven
Squares	Big Bad Numbers

Step Eight	Step Nine	Step Ten
6 Sixes	**7** Sevens	**8** Eights

Action Plan & Success Tracker

Complete each activity in the order shown below.　　✓

A. **Speed Builder #1** (Pre-Test) page 24	
B. **Memory Builder** page 25	
C. Study Cards & **Speed Builder #2** (Take a break now.) page 24	
D. Study Cards & **Speed Builder #3** page 24	
E. Study Cards & **Distributed Practice** (at home) page 27	
Speed Builder #4: Wait until the next day.	
F. Study Cards & **Speed Builder #4** (Final) page 24	

TEACHERS: If using a two-day pacing, assign the Extra **Memory Builder** here, before starting Activity D. The Extra Memory Builder is found in the teacher edition on page 85.

Name_____

4 Fours

Speed Builders: Fours

Goal: Show improvement after each Speed Builder. Score 100% correct by Speed Builder #4 (next day).
Target Time: One minute per column. Adjust time only if necessary.
Directions: Go in order, and do not skip around. If you don't recall a fact within two seconds, move on to the next problem.

Speed Builder #1
Pre-Test

2 x 4 = _____
5 x 4 = _____
7 x 4 = _____
9 x 4 = _____
6 x 4 = _____

5 x 4 = _____
9 x 4 = _____
2 x 4 = _____
7 x 4 = _____
4 x 4 = _____

6 x 4 = _____
3 x 4 = _____
8 x 4 = _____
5 x 4 = _____
9 x 4 = _____

3 x 4 = _____
2 x 4 = _____
8 x 4 = _____
4 x 4 = _____
7 x 4 = _____

6 x 4 = _____
8 x 4 = _____
3 x 4 = _____
4 x 4 = _____
7 x 4 = _____

3 x 4 = _____
2 x 4 = _____
5 x 4 = _____
4 x 4 = _____
6 x 4 = _____

9 x 4 = _____
8 x 4 = _____
6 x 4 = _____
3 x 4 = _____
2 x 4 = _____

NEXT: Memory Builder & Study Cards

FOLD along dotted line to hide previous answers.

Speed Builder #2
Practice

4 x 2 = _____
4 x 5 = _____
4 x 7 = _____
4 x 9 = _____
4 x 6 = _____

4 x 5 = _____
4 x 9 = _____
4 x 2 = _____
4 x 7 = _____
4 x 4 = _____

4 x 6 = _____
4 x 3 = _____
4 x 8 = _____
4 x 5 = _____
4 x 9 = _____

4 x 3 = _____
4 x 2 = _____
4 x 8 = _____
4 x 4 = _____
4 x 7 = _____

4 x 6 = _____
4 x 8 = _____
4 x 3 = _____
4 x 4 = _____
4 x 7 = _____

4 x 3 = _____
4 x 2 = _____
4 x 5 = _____
4 x 4 = _____
4 x 6 = _____

4 x 9 = _____
4 x 8 = _____
4 x 6 = _____
4 x 3 = _____
4 x 2 = _____

NEXT AFTER (BREAK): Extra Memory Builder (if using two-day pacing) & Study Cards

FOLD along dotted line to hide previous answers.

Speed Builder #3
Practice

2 x 4 = _____
5 x 4 = _____
7 x 4 = _____
9 x 4 = _____
6 x 4 = _____

5 x 4 = _____
9 x 4 = _____
2 x 4 = _____
7 x 4 = _____
4 x 4 = _____

6 x 4 = _____
3 x 4 = _____
8 x 4 = _____
5 x 4 = _____
9 x 4 = _____

3 x 4 = _____
2 x 4 = _____
8 x 4 = _____
4 x 4 = _____
7 x 4 = _____

6 x 4 = _____
8 x 4 = _____
3 x 4 = _____
4 x 4 = _____
7 x 4 = _____

3 x 4 = _____
2 x 4 = _____
5 x 4 = _____
4 x 4 = _____
6 x 4 = _____

9 x 4 = _____
8 x 4 = _____
6 x 4 = _____
3 x 4 = _____
2 x 4 = _____

NEXT: Distributed Practice (at home) & Study Cards

FOLD along dotted line to hide previous answers.

Speed Builder #4
FINAL (taken the next day)

4 x 2 = _____
4 x 5 = _____
4 x 7 = _____
4 x 9 = _____
4 x 6 = _____

4 x 5 = _____
4 x 9 = _____
4 x 2 = _____
4 x 7 = _____
4 x 4 = _____

4 x 6 = _____
4 x 3 = _____
4 x 8 = _____
4 x 5 = _____
4 x 9 = _____

4 x 3 = _____
4 x 2 = _____
4 x 8 = _____
4 x 4 = _____
4 x 7 = _____

4 x 6 = _____
4 x 8 = _____
4 x 3 = _____
4 x 4 = _____
4 x 7 = _____

4 x 3 = _____
4 x 2 = _____
4 x 5 = _____
4 x 4 = _____
4 x 6 = _____

4 x 9 = _____
4 x 8 = _____
4 x 6 = _____
4 x 3 = _____
4 x 2 = _____

Pre-Test Score:_____/35   Practice Score: _____/35   Practice Score: _____/35   **FINAL Score:** _____/35

Memory Builder: Fours

Name_____

Directions: Complete each row in order from left to right. **Do not skip around.**

Two-Second Clock: `00:00:02`
If you don't recall a fact within two seconds, **flip the page for a hint.**

Cover up your Speed Builder results. Do not use any other hints, including multiplication tables, calculators, finger counting, tally marks, Refresher Posters, etc.

Focus Facts: Row 1: the digits ①, ④, and ⑦ multiplied by 4
Row 2: the digits ②, ⑤, and ⑧ multiplied by 4
Row 3: the digits ③, ⑥, and ⑨ multiplied by 4

Row 1 Focus Facts: the digits ①, ④, and ⑦ multiplied by 4

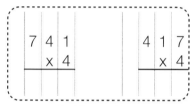

3-2-1 Memory Building System – First **three** problems: OK to flip the page for a hint.

Next **two** problems: Try not to flip the page.

Last **one:** Know facts by heart.

Row 2 Focus Facts: the digits ②, ⑤, and ⑧ multiplied by 4

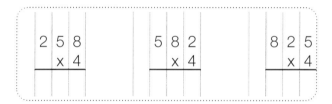

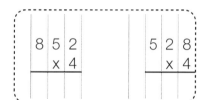

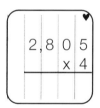

Row 3 Focus Facts: the digits ③, ⑥, and ⑨ multiplied by 4

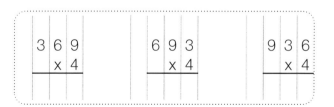

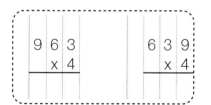

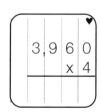

STUDENTS: Be sure to correct all mistakes.

Final Score: _____/18

Next Activity
Study Cards (in Student Edition) & Speed Builder #2, p. 24

Step Three

4

Fours

**Here's
your hint.**

Multiples
of four

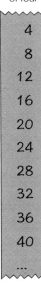

4
8
12
16
20
24
28
32
36
40
...

Make sure this page is hidden/covered and not easily seen when working on the *Memory Builders* and *Distributed Practice.*

With your pencil, touch the multiples of four in the correct order from top to bottom while saying,

"One time,"
"two times,"
"three times,"

and so on until you reach the multiple that you're looking for.

Memorize it, flip the page over, and continue working.

Do not write any other hints on this page.

As you rehearse, the facts will move from your short-term memory into your long-term memory.

4
Fours

Name_____

Distributed Practice: Fours

Distributed Practice means spacing your practice sessions out over time in order to improve learning. It is the opposite of cramming.

Directions: Complete each row in order from left to right. **Do not skip around.**

Two-Second Clock: `00:00:02`
If you don't recall a fact within two seconds, **flip the page for a hint.**

Remember to cover up the hint page from the Memory Builder. Do not use multiplication tables, calculators, finger counting, tally marks, Refresher Posters, etc.

Focus Facts: Row 1: the digits ⑨, ⑥, and ① multiplied by 4
Row 2: the digits ⑧, ⑤, and ③ multiplied by 4
Row 3: the digits ⑦, ④, and ② multiplied by 4

Row 1 Focus Facts: the digits ⑨, ⑥, and ① multiplied by 4

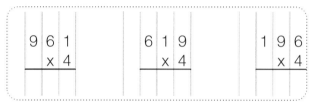
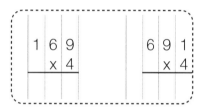
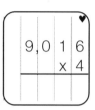

3-2-1 Memory Building System – First **three** problems: OK to flip the page for a hint.

Next **two** problems: Try not to flip the page.

Last **one:** Know facts by heart.

Row 2 Focus Facts: the digits ⑧, ⑤, and ③ multiplied by 4

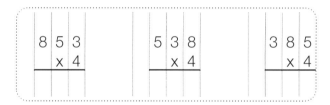
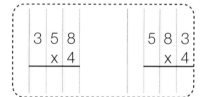
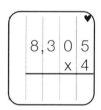

Row 3 Focus Facts: the digits ⑦, ④, and ② multiplied by 4

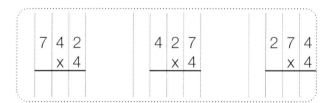
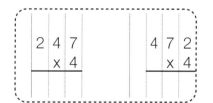
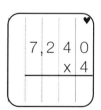

STUDENTS: Be sure to correct all mistakes.

Final Score: _____/18

Next Activity (Next Day)
Study Cards (in Student Edition)
& Speed Builder #4, p. 24

**Here's
your hint.**

Multiples
of four

4
8
12
16
20
24
28
32
36
40
...

Make sure this page is hidden/covered and not easily seen when working on the **Memory Builders** and **Distributed Practice.**

With your pencil, touch the multiples of four in the correct order from top to bottom while saying,

> **"One time,"**
> **"two times,"**
> **"three times,"**

and so on until you reach the multiple that you're looking for.

Memorize it, flip the page over, and continue working.

Do not write any other hints on this page.

As you rehearse, the facts will move from your short-term memory into your long-term memory.

Reveal the Pattern: Fours

The multiples of four have created a secret hidden pattern in the Hundred Chart below. Reveal the pattern by **counting by four** and shading in the correct boxes. The first two have been done for you.

1	2	3	4	5	6	7	8	9	10
11	12	13	14	15	16	17	18	19	20
21	22	23	24	25	26	27	28	29	30
31	32	33	34	35	36	37	38	39	40
41	42	43	44	45	46	47	48	49	50
51	52	53	54	55	56	57	58	59	60
61	62	63	64	65	66	67	68	69	70
71	72	73	74	75	76	77	78	79	80
81	82	83	84	85	86	87	88	89	90
91	92	93	94	95	96	97	98	99	100

Step Four
The Fives

Magic Sequence Navigator
10 Powerful Steps to Multiplication Fluency

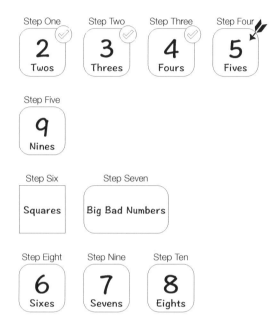

Step One
2
Twos ✓

Step Two
3
Threes ✓

Step Three
4
Fours ✓

Step Four
5
Fives

Step Five
9
Nines

Step Six
Squares

Step Seven
Big Bad Numbers

Step Eight
6
Sixes

Step Nine
7
Sevens

Step Ten
8
Eights

Action Plan & Success Tracker
Complete each activity in the order shown below. ✓

A. **Speed Builder #1** (Pre-Test) page 30	
B. **Memory Builder** page 31	
C. Study Cards & **Speed Builder #2** page 30	
Take a break now.	
D. Study Cards & **Speed Builder #3** page 30	
E. Study Cards & **Distributed Practice** (at home) page 33	
Speed Builder #4: Wait until the next day.	
F. Study Cards & **Speed Builder #4** (Final) page 30	

TEACHERS: If using a two-day pacing, assign the Extra **Memory Builder** here, before starting Activity D. The Extra Memory Builder is found in the teacher edition on page 87.

5 Fives
Speed Builders: Fives

Goal: Show improvement after each Speed Builder. Score 100% correct by Speed Builder #4 (next day).
Target Time: One minute per column. Adjust time only if necessary.
Directions: Go in order, and do not skip around. If you don't recall a fact within two seconds, move on to the next problem.

Name_____

Speed Builder #1
Pre-Test

2 x 5 = _____
5 x 5 = _____
7 x 5 = _____
9 x 5 = _____
6 x 5 = _____

5 x 5 = _____
9 x 5 = _____
2 x 5 = _____
7 x 5 = _____
4 x 5 = _____

6 x 5 = _____
3 x 5 = _____
8 x 5 = _____
5 x 5 = _____
9 x 5 = _____

3 x 5 = _____
2 x 5 = _____
8 x 5 = _____
4 x 5 = _____
7 x 5 = _____

6 x 5 = _____
8 x 5 = _____
3 x 5 = _____
4 x 5 = _____
7 x 5 = _____

3 x 5 = _____
2 x 5 = _____
5 x 5 = _____
4 x 5 = _____
6 x 5 = _____

9 x 5 = _____
8 x 5 = _____
6 x 5 = _____
3 x 5 = _____
2 x 5 = _____

Pre-Test Score:_____/35

NEXT: Memory Builder & Study Cards

FOLD along dotted line to hide previous answers.

Speed Builder #2
Practice

5 x 2 = _____
5 x 5 = _____
5 x 7 = _____
5 x 9 = _____
5 x 6 = _____

5 x 5 = _____
5 x 9 = _____
5 x 2 = _____
5 x 7 = _____
5 x 4 = _____

5 x 6 = _____
5 x 3 = _____
5 x 8 = _____
5 x 5 = _____
5 x 9 = _____

5 x 3 = _____
5 x 2 = _____
5 x 8 = _____
5 x 4 = _____
5 x 7 = _____

5 x 6 = _____
5 x 8 = _____
5 x 3 = _____
5 x 4 = _____
5 x 7 = _____

5 x 3 = _____
5 x 2 = _____
5 x 5 = _____
5 x 4 = _____
5 x 6 = _____

5 x 9 = _____
5 x 8 = _____
5 x 6 = _____
5 x 3 = _____
5 x 2 = _____

Practice Score: _____/35

NEXT AFTER (BREAK): Extra Memory Builder (if using two-day pacing) & Study Cards

FOLD along dotted line to hide previous answers.

Speed Builder #3
Practice

2 x 5 = _____
5 x 5 = _____
7 x 5 = _____
9 x 5 = _____
6 x 5 = _____

5 x 5 = _____
9 x 5 = _____
2 x 5 = _____
7 x 5 = _____
4 x 5 = _____

6 x 5 = _____
3 x 5 = _____
8 x 5 = _____
5 x 5 = _____
9 x 5 = _____

3 x 5 = _____
2 x 5 = _____
8 x 5 = _____
4 x 5 = _____
7 x 5 = _____

6 x 5 = _____
8 x 5 = _____
3 x 5 = _____
4 x 5 = _____
7 x 5 = _____

3 x 5 = _____
2 x 5 = _____
5 x 5 = _____
4 x 5 = _____
6 x 5 = _____

9 x 5 = _____
8 x 5 = _____
6 x 5 = _____
3 x 5 = _____
2 x 5 = _____

Practice Score: _____/35

NEXT: Distributed Practice (at home) & Study Cards

FOLD along dotted line to hide previous answers.

Speed Builder #4
FINAL (taken the next day)

5 x 2 = _____
5 x 5 = _____
5 x 7 = _____
5 x 9 = _____
5 x 6 = _____

5 x 5 = _____
5 x 9 = _____
5 x 2 = _____
5 x 7 = _____
5 x 4 = _____

5 x 6 = _____
5 x 3 = _____
5 x 8 = _____
5 x 5 = _____
5 x 9 = _____

5 x 3 = _____
5 x 2 = _____
5 x 8 = _____
5 x 4 = _____
5 x 7 = _____

5 x 6 = _____
5 x 8 = _____
5 x 3 = _____
5 x 4 = _____
5 x 7 = _____

5 x 3 = _____
5 x 2 = _____
5 x 5 = _____
5 x 4 = _____
5 x 6 = _____

5 x 9 = _____
5 x 8 = _____
5 x 6 = _____
5 x 3 = _____
5 x 2 = _____

FINAL Score: _____/35

5 Fives
Memory Builder: Fives

Directions: Complete each row in order from left to right. **Do not skip around.**

Two-Second Clock: `00:00:02`
If you don't recall a fact within two seconds, **flip the page for a hint.**

Cover up your Speed Builder results. Do not use any other hints, including multiplication tables, calculators, finger counting, tally marks, Refresher Posters, etc.

Focus Facts: Row 1: the digits ①, ④, and ⑦ multiplied by 5
Row 2: the digits ②, ⑤, and ⑧ multiplied by 5
Row 3: the digits ③, ⑥, and ⑨ multiplied by 5

Row 1 Focus Facts: the digits ①, ④, and ⑦ multiplied by 5

1 4 7 × 5	4 7 1 × 5	7 1 4 × 5

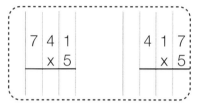

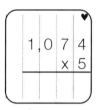

3-2-1 Memory Building System – First **three** problems: OK to flip the page for a hint.

Next **two** problems: Try not to flip the page.

Last **one:** Know facts by heart.

Row 2 Focus Facts: the digits ②, ⑤, and ⑧ multiplied by 5

2 5 8 × 5	5 8 2 × 5	8 2 5 × 5

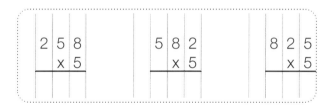

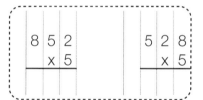

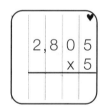

Row 3 Focus Facts: the digits ③, ⑥, and ⑨ multiplied by 5

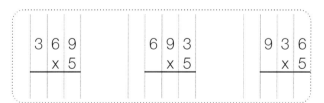

3 6 9 × 5	6 9 3 × 5	9 3 6 × 5

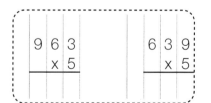

STUDENTS: Be sure to correct all mistakes.

Final Score: _____ /18

Next Activity
Study Cards (in Student Edition) & Speed Builder #2, p. 30

Step Four

5

Fives

**Here's
your hint.**

Multiples
of five

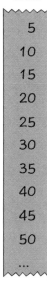

5
10
15
20
25
30
35
40
45
50
...

Make sure this page is hidden/covered and not easily seen when working on the **Memory Builders** and **Distributed Practice.**

With your pencil, touch the multiples of five in the correct order from top to bottom while saying,

> *"One time,"*
> *"two times,"*
> *"three times,"*

and so on until you reach the multiple that you're looking for.

Memorize it, flip the page over, and continue working.

Do not write any other hints on this page.

As you rehearse, the facts will move from your short-term memory into your long-term memory.

5 Fives
Distributed Practice: Fives

Distributed Practice means spacing your practice sessions out over time in order to improve learning. It is the opposite of cramming.

Directions: Complete each row in order from left to right. ***Do not skip around.***

Two-Second Clock: `00:00:02`
If you don't recall a fact within two seconds, ***flip the page for a hint.***

Remember to cover up the hint page from the Memory Builder.
Do not use multiplication tables, calculators, finger counting, tally marks, Refresher Posters, etc.

Focus Facts: Row 1: the digits (9), (6), and (1) multiplied by 5
Row 2: the digits (8), (5), and (3) multiplied by 5
Row 3: the digits (7), (4), and (2) multiplied by 5

Row 1 Focus Facts: the digits (9), (6), and (1) multiplied by 5

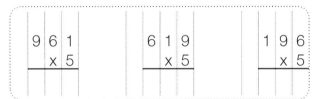

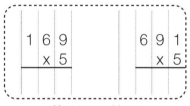

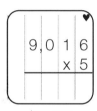

3-2-1 Memory Building System – First ***three*** problems: OK to flip the page for a hint.

Next ***two*** problems: Try not to flip the page.

Last ***one:*** Know facts by heart.

Row 2 Focus Facts: the digits (8), (5), and (3) multiplied by 5

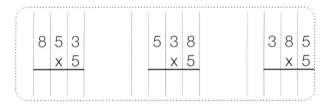

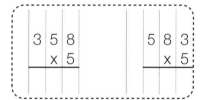

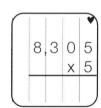

Row 3 Focus Facts: the digits (7), (4), and (2) multiplied by 5

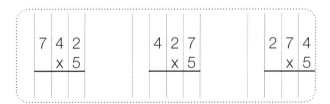

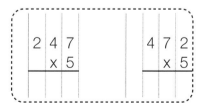

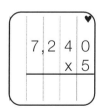

STUDENTS: Be sure to correct all mistakes.

Final Score: _____ /18

Next Activity (Next Day)
Study Cards (in Student Edition) & Speed Builder #4, p. 30

Step Four

Fives

Here's your hint.

Multiples of five

5
10
15
20
25
30
35
40
45
50
...

Make sure this page is hidden/covered and not easily seen when working on the **Memory Builders** and **Distributed Practice.**

With your pencil, touch the multiples of five in the correct order from top to bottom while saying,

"One time,"
"two times,"
"three times,"

and so on until you reach the multiple that you're looking for.

Memorize it, flip the page over, and continue working.

Do not write any other hints on this page.

As you rehearse, the facts will move from your short-term memory into your long-term memory.

Reveal the Pattern: Fives

The multiples of five have created a secret hidden pattern in the Hundred Chart below. Reveal the pattern by **counting by five** and shading in the correct boxes. The first two have been done for you.

1	2	3	4	5	6	7	8	9	10
11	12	13	14	15	16	17	18	19	20
21	22	23	24	25	26	27	28	29	30
31	32	33	34	35	36	37	38	39	40
41	42	43	44	45	46	47	48	49	50
51	52	53	54	55	56	57	58	59	60
61	62	63	64	65	66	67	68	69	70
71	72	73	74	75	76	77	78	79	80
81	82	83	84	85	86	87	88	89	90
91	92	93	94	95	96	97	98	99	100

Step Five
The Nines

Magic Sequence Navigator

10 Powerful Steps to Multiplication Fluency

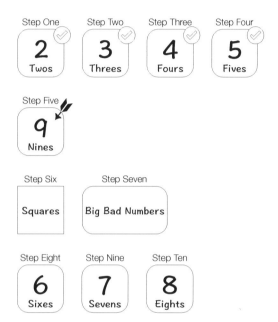

Action Plan & Success Tracker

Complete each activity in the order shown below. ✓

A. **Speed Builder #1** (Pre-Test) page 36	
B. **Memory Builder** page 37	
C. Study Cards & **Speed Builder #2** Take a break now. page 36	
D. Study Cards & **Speed Builder #3** page 36	
E. Study Cards & **Distributed Practice** (at home) page 39	
Speed Builder #4: Wait until the next day.	
F. Study Cards & **Speed Builder #4** (Final) page 36	

TEACHERS: If using a two-day pacing, assign the Extra **Memory Builder** here, before starting Activity D. The Extra Memory Builder is found in the teacher edition on page 89.

Speed Builders: Nines

9 Nines

Name_____

Goal: Show improvement after each Speed Builder. Score 100% correct by Speed Builder #4 (next day).
Target Time: One minute per column. Adjust time only if necessary.
Directions: Go in order, and do not skip around. If you don't recall a fact within two seconds, move on to the next problem.

Speed Builder #1
Pre-Test

2 x 9 = _____
5 x 9 = _____
7 x 9 = _____
9 x 9 = _____
6 x 9 = _____

5 x 9 = _____
9 x 9 = _____
2 x 9 = _____
7 x 9 = _____
4 x 9 = _____

6 x 9 = _____
3 x 9 = _____
8 x 9 = _____
5 x 9 = _____
9 x 9 = _____

3 x 9 = _____
2 x 9 = _____
8 x 9 = _____
4 x 9 = _____
7 x 9 = _____

6 x 9 = _____
8 x 9 = _____
3 x 9 = _____
4 x 9 = _____
7 x 9 = _____

3 x 9 = _____
2 x 9 = _____
5 x 9 = _____
4 x 9 = _____
6 x 9 = _____

9 x 9 = _____
8 x 9 = _____
6 x 9 = _____
3 x 9 = _____
2 x 9 = _____

Pre-Test Score:_____/35

NEXT: Memory Builder & Study Cards

FOLD along dotted line to hide previous answers.

Speed Builder #2
Practice

9 x 2 = _____
9 x 5 = _____
9 x 7 = _____
9 x 9 = _____
9 x 6 = _____

9 x 5 = _____
9 x 9 = _____
9 x 2 = _____
9 x 7 = _____
9 x 4 = _____

9 x 6 = _____
9 x 3 = _____
9 x 8 = _____
9 x 5 = _____
9 x 9 = _____

9 x 3 = _____
9 x 2 = _____
9 x 8 = _____
9 x 4 = _____
9 x 7 = _____

9 x 6 = _____
9 x 8 = _____
9 x 3 = _____
9 x 4 = _____
9 x 7 = _____

9 x 3 = _____
9 x 2 = _____
9 x 5 = _____
9 x 4 = _____
9 x 6 = _____

9 x 9 = _____
9 x 8 = _____
9 x 6 = _____
9 x 3 = _____
9 x 2 = _____

Practice Score: _____/35

NEXT AFTER (BREAK): Extra Memory Builder (if using two-day pacing) & Study Cards

FOLD along dotted line to hide previous answers.

Speed Builder #3
Practice

2 x 9 = _____
5 x 9 = _____
7 x 9 = _____
9 x 9 = _____
6 x 9 = _____

5 x 9 = _____
9 x 9 = _____
2 x 9 = _____
7 x 9 = _____
4 x 9 = _____

6 x 9 = _____
3 x 9 = _____
8 x 9 = _____
5 x 9 = _____
9 x 9 = _____

3 x 9 = _____
2 x 9 = _____
8 x 9 = _____
4 x 9 = _____
7 x 9 = _____

6 x 9 = _____
8 x 9 = _____
3 x 9 = _____
4 x 9 = _____
7 x 9 = _____

3 x 9 = _____
2 x 9 = _____
5 x 9 = _____
4 x 9 = _____
6 x 9 = _____

9 x 9 = _____
8 x 9 = _____
6 x 9 = _____
3 x 9 = _____
2 x 9 = _____

Practice Score: _____/35

NEXT: Distributed Practice (at home) & Study Cards

FOLD along dotted line to hide previous answers.

Speed Builder #4
FINAL (taken the next day)

9 x 2 = _____
9 x 5 = _____
9 x 7 = _____
9 x 9 = _____
9 x 6 = _____

9 x 5 = _____
9 x 9 = _____
9 x 2 = _____
9 x 7 = _____
9 x 4 = _____

9 x 6 = _____
9 x 3 = _____
9 x 8 = _____
9 x 5 = _____
9 x 9 = _____

9 x 3 = _____
9 x 2 = _____
9 x 8 = _____
9 x 4 = _____
9 x 7 = _____

9 x 6 = _____
9 x 8 = _____
9 x 3 = _____
9 x 4 = _____
9 x 7 = _____

9 x 3 = _____
9 x 2 = _____
9 x 5 = _____
9 x 4 = _____
9 x 6 = _____

9 x 9 = _____
9 x 8 = _____
9 x 6 = _____
9 x 3 = _____
9 x 2 = _____

FINAL Score: _____/35

Memory Builder: Nines

Name_____

Directions: Complete each row in order from left to right. **Do not skip around.**

Two-Second Clock: `00:00:02`
If you don't recall a fact within two seconds, **flip the page for a hint.**

Cover up your Speed Builder results. Do not use any other hints, including multiplication tables, calculators, finger counting, tally marks, Refresher Posters, etc.

Focus Facts:
Row 1: the digits ①, ④, and ⑦ multiplied by 9
Row 2: the digits ②, ⑤, and ⑧ multiplied by 9
Row 3: the digits ③, ⑥, and ⑨ multiplied by 9

Row 1 Focus Facts: the digits ①, ④, and ⑦ multiplied by 9

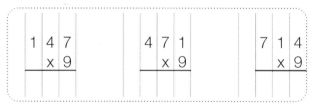

3-2-1 Memory Building System – First **three** problems: OK to flip the page for a hint.

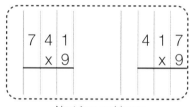

Next **two** problems: Try not to flip the page.

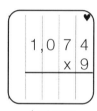

Last **one:** Know facts by heart.

Row 2 Focus Facts: the digits ②, ⑤, and ⑧ multiplied by 9

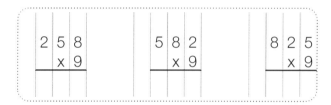

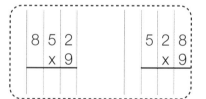

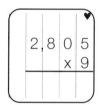

Row 3 Focus Facts: the digits ③, ⑥, and ⑨ multiplied by 9

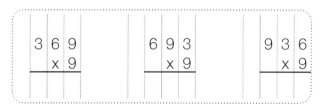

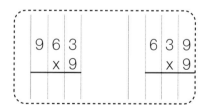

STUDENTS: Be sure to correct all mistakes.

Final Score: _____/18

Next Activity
Study Cards (in Student Edition)
& Speed Builder #2, p. 36

Step Five

9
Nines

**Here's
your hint.**

↓

Magic Box

1	2	3	4
8	7	6	5

↓ ↓ ↓ ↓
18 27 36 45
81 72 63 54

Make sure this page is hidden/covered and not easily seen when working on the **Memory Builders** and **Distributed Practice.**

When multiplying 9 by a single digit number from 2 to 9, "Think One Less," then use the Magic Box.

Example: 9 x 3 = ____

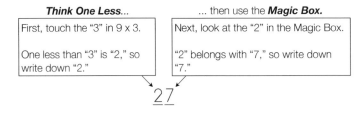

Think One Less...

First, touch the "3" in 9 x 3.

One less than "3" is "2," so write down "2."

... then use the **Magic Box.**

Next, look at the "2" in the Magic Box.

"2" belongs with "7," so write down "7."

27

Answer: 9 x 3 = 27

Memorize it, flip the page over, and continue working.

Do not write any other hints on this page.

As you rehearse, the facts will move from your short-term memory into your long-term memory.

Distributed Practice: Nines

Distributed Practice means spacing your practice sessions out over time in order to improve learning. It is the opposite of cramming.

Directions: Complete each row in order from left to right. ***Do not skip around.***

Two-Second Clock: ⸨00:00:02⸩
If you don't recall a fact within two seconds, *flip the page for a hint.*

Remember to cover up the hint page from the Memory Builder. Do not use multiplication tables, calculators, finger counting, tally marks, Refresher Posters, etc.

Focus Facts: Row 1: the digits ⑨, ⑥, and ① multiplied by 9
Row 2: the digits ⑧, ⑤, and ③ multiplied by 9
Row 3: the digits ⑦, ④, and ② multiplied by 9

Magic Box

Row 1 Focus Facts: the digits ⑨, ⑥, and ① multiplied by 9

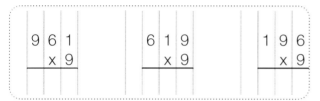

3-2-1 Memory Building System – First ***three*** problems: OK to flip the page for a hint.

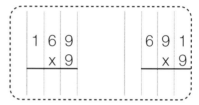

Next ***two*** problems: Try not to flip the page.

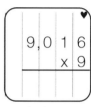

Last ***one:*** Know facts by heart.

Row 2 Focus Facts: the digits ⑧, ⑤, and ③ multiplied by 9

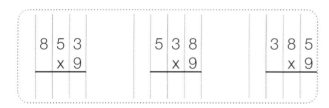

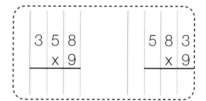

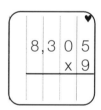

Row 3 Focus Facts: the digits ⑦, ④, and ② multiplied by 9

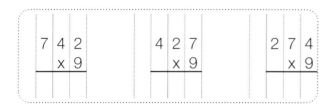

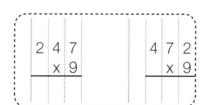

STUDENTS: Be sure to correct all mistakes.

Final Score: _____/18

Next Activity (Next Day)
Study Cards (in Student Edition) & Speed Builder #4, p. 36

9

Nines

**Here's
your hint.**

↓

Magic Box

1	2	3	4
8	7	6	5

↓ ↓ ↓ ↓
18 27 36 45
81 72 63 54

Make sure this page is hidden/covered and not easily seen when working on the **Memory Builders** and **Distributed Practice.**

When multiplying 9 by a single digit number from 2 to 9, "Think One Less," then use the Magic Box.

Example: 9 x 3 = ____

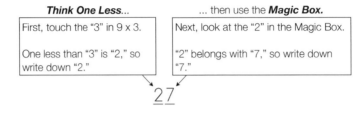

Think One Less...	... then use the **Magic Box.**
First, touch the "3" in 9 x 3. One less than "3" is "2," so write down "2."	Next, look at the "2" in the Magic Box. "2" belongs with "7," so write down "7."

2 7

Answer: 9 x 3 = 27

Memorize it, flip the page over, and continue working.

Do not write any other hints on this page.

As you rehearse, the facts will move from your short-term memory into your long-term memory.

Reveal the Pattern: Nines

The multiples of nine have created a secret hidden pattern in the Hundred Chart below. Reveal the pattern by **counting by nine** and shading in the correct boxes. The first one has been done for you.

1	2	3	4	5	6	7	8	9	10
11	12	13	14	15	16	17	18	19	20
21	22	23	24	25	26	27	28	29	30
31	32	33	34	35	36	37	38	39	40
41	42	43	44	45	46	47	48	49	50
51	52	53	54	55	56	57	58	59	60
61	62	63	64	65	66	67	68	69	70
71	72	73	74	75	76	77	78	79	80
81	82	83	84	85	86	87	88	89	90
91	92	93	94	95	96	97	98	99	100

The Squares

Magic Sequence Navigator

10 Powerful Steps to Multiplication Fluency

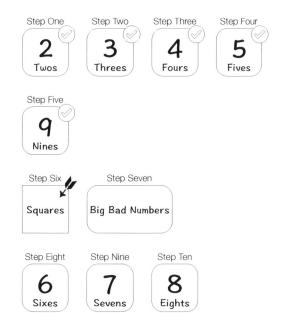

Step One
2
Twos ✓

Step Two
3
Threes ✓

Step Three
4
Fours ✓

Step Four
5
Fives ✓

Step Five
9
Nines ✓

Step Six ✎
Squares

Step Seven
Big Bad Numbers

Step Eight
6
Sixes

Step Nine
7
Sevens

Step Ten
8
Eights

Action Plan & Success Tracker

Complete each activity in the order shown below.   ✓

A. Speed Builder #1 (Pre-Test) page 42	
B. Memory Builder page 43	
C. Study Cards & **Speed Builder #2** page 42	
D. Study Cards & **Speed Builder #3** page 42	
E. Study Cards & **Distributed Practice** (at home) page 45	
Speed Builder #4: Wait until the next day.	
F. Study Cards & **Speed Builder #4** (Final) page 42	

Take a break now.

Teachers: If using a two-day pacing, assign the Extra **Memory Builder** here, before starting Activity D. Extra Memory Builders are found in the teacher edition starting on page 91.

Speed Builders: Squares

Goal: Show improvement after each Speed Builder. Score 100% correct by Speed Builder #4 (next day).
Target Time: One minute per column. Adjust time only if necessary.
Directions: Go in order, and do not skip around. If you don't recall a fact within two seconds, move on to the next problem.

Speed Builder #1
Pre-Test

2 x 2 = _____
5 x 5 = _____
7 x 7 = _____
9 x 9 = _____
6 x 6 = _____

5 x 5 = _____
9 x 9 = _____
2 x 2 = _____
7 x 7 = _____
4 x 4 = _____

6 x 6 = _____
3 x 3 = _____
8 x 8 = _____
5 x 5 = _____
9 x 9 = _____

3 x 3 = _____
2 x 2 = _____
8 x 8 = _____
4 x 4 = _____
7 x 7 = _____

6 x 6 = _____
8 x 8 = _____
3 x 3 = _____
4 x 4 = _____
7 x 7 = _____

3 x 3 = _____
2 x 2 = _____
5 x 5 = _____
4 x 4 = _____
6 x 6 = _____

9 x 9 = _____
8 x 8 = _____
6 x 6 = _____
3 x 3 = _____
2 x 2 = _____

Speed Builder #2
Practice

2 x 2 = _____
5 x 5 = _____
7 x 7 = _____
9 x 9 = _____
6 x 6 = _____

5 x 5 = _____
9 x 9 = _____
2 x 2 = _____
7 x 7 = _____
4 x 4 = _____

6 x 6 = _____
3 x 3 = _____
8 x 8 = _____
5 x 5 = _____
9 x 9 = _____

3 x 3 = _____
2 x 2 = _____
8 x 8 = _____
4 x 4 = _____
7 x 7 = _____

6 x 6 = _____
8 x 8 = _____
3 x 3 = _____
4 x 4 = _____
7 x 7 = _____

3 x 3 = _____
2 x 2 = _____
5 x 5 = _____
4 x 4 = _____
6 x 6 = _____

9 x 9 = _____
8 x 8 = _____
6 x 6 = _____
3 x 3 = _____
2 x 2 = _____

Speed Builder #3
Practice

2 x 2 = _____
5 x 5 = _____
7 x 7 = _____
9 x 9 = _____
6 x 6 = _____

5 x 5 = _____
9 x 9 = _____
2 x 2 = _____
7 x 7 = _____
4 x 4 = _____

6 x 6 = _____
3 x 3 = _____
8 x 8 = _____
5 x 5 = _____
9 x 9 = _____

3 x 3 = _____
2 x 2 = _____
8 x 8 = _____
4 x 4 = _____
7 x 7 = _____

6 x 6 = _____
8 x 8 = _____
3 x 3 = _____
4 x 4 = _____
7 x 7 = _____

3 x 3 = _____
2 x 2 = _____
5 x 5 = _____
4 x 4 = _____
6 x 6 = _____

9 x 9 = _____
8 x 8 = _____
6 x 6 = _____
3 x 3 = _____
2 x 2 = _____

Speed Builder #4
FINAL (taken the next day)

2 x 2 = _____
5 x 5 = _____
7 x 7 = _____
9 x 9 = _____
6 x 6 = _____

5 x 5 = _____
9 x 9 = _____
2 x 2 = _____
7 x 7 = _____
4 x 4 = _____

6 x 6 = _____
3 x 3 = _____
8 x 8 = _____
5 x 5 = _____
9 x 9 = _____

3 x 3 = _____
2 x 2 = _____
8 x 8 = _____
4 x 4 = _____
7 x 7 = _____

6 x 6 = _____
8 x 8 = _____
3 x 3 = _____
4 x 4 = _____
7 x 7 = _____

3 x 3 = _____
2 x 2 = _____
5 x 5 = _____
4 x 4 = _____
6 x 6 = _____

9 x 9 = _____
8 x 8 = _____
6 x 6 = _____
3 x 3 = _____
2 x 2 = _____

NEXT: Memory Builder & Study Cards

NEXT AFTER BREAK: Extra Memory Builder (if using two-day pacing) & Study Cards

NEXT: Distributed Practice (at home) & Study Cards

FOLD along dotted line to hide previous answers.

FOLD along dotted line to hide previous answers.

FOLD along dotted line to hide previous answers.

Pre-Test Score:_____ /35

Practice Score: _____ /35

Practice Score: _____ /35

FINAL Score: _____ **/35**

Squares

Memory Builder: Squares

Name_____

Directions: Complete each row in order from left to right. **Do not skip around.**

Focus Facts: Row 1: the digits ①, ④, and ⑦ squared
Row 2: the digits ②, ⑤, and ⑧ squared
Row 3: the digits ③, ⑥, and ⑨ squared

Two-Second Clock: `00:00:02`
If you don't recall a fact within two seconds, **flip the page for a hint.**

Cover up your Speed Builder results. Do not use any other hints, including multiplication tables, calculators, finger counting, tally marks, Refresher Posters, etc.

Row 1 Focus Facts: the digits ①, ④, and ⑦ squared

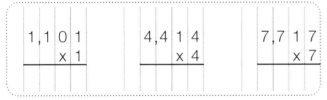

3-3 Memory Building System – First **three** problems: OK to flip the page for a hint.

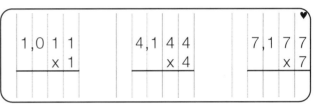

Last **three** problems: Know the facts by heart.

Row 2 Focus Facts: the digits ②, ⑤, and ⑧ squared

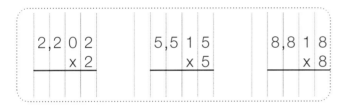

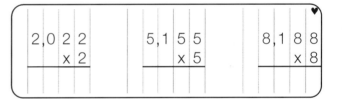

Row 3 Focus Facts: the digits ③, ⑥, and ⑨ squared

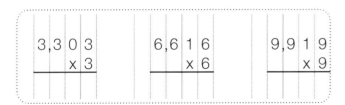

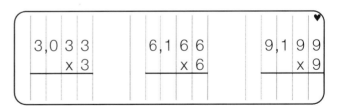

STUDENTS: Be sure to correct all mistakes.

Final Score: _____/18

Next Activity
Study Cards (in Student Edition)
& Speed Builder #2, p. 42

Squares

Here's your hint.

↓

1 x 1 = 1
2 x 2 = 4
3 x 3 = 9
4 x 4 = 16
5 x 5 = 25
NEW> 6 x 6 = **36** six, six, thirty-six (a rhyme)
NEW> 7 x 7 = **49** Sevens Twins forgot a star
NEW> 8 x 8 = **64** Nintendo 64
9 x 9 = 81

Make sure this page is hidden/covered and not easily seen when working on the **Memory Builders** and **Distributed Practice.**

Use the mnemonic devices to the left to memorize the Squares. Flip the page and keep working.

Do not write any other hints on this page.

As you rehearse, the facts will move from your short-term memory into your long-term memory.

Name_____

Distributed Practice: Squares

Distributed Practice means spacing your practice sessions out over time in order to improve learning. It is the opposite of cramming.

Directions: Complete each row in order from left to right. **Do not skip around.**

Focus Facts: Row 1: the digits ①, ④, and ⑦ squared
Row 2: the digits ②, ⑤, and ⑧ squared
Row 3: the digits ③, ⑥, and ⑨ squared

Two-Second Clock: `00:00:02`
If you don't recall a fact within two seconds, **flip the page for a hint.**

Remember to cover up the hint page from the Memory Builder.
Do not use multiplication tables, calculators, finger counting, tally marks, Refresher Posters, etc.

Row 1 Focus Facts: the digits ①, ④, and ⑦ squared

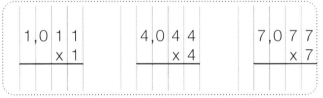

3-3 Memory Building System – First *three* problems: OK to flip the page for a hint.

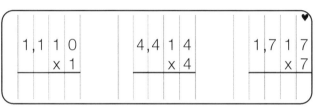

Last *three* problems: Know the facts by heart.

Row 2 Focus Facts: the digits ②, ⑤, and ⑧ squared

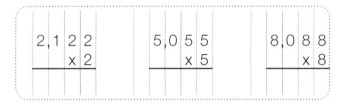

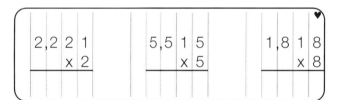

Row 3 Focus Facts: the digits ③, ⑥, and ⑨ squared

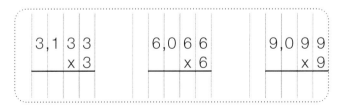

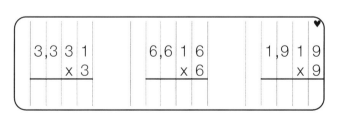

STUDENTS: Be sure to correct all mistakes.

Final Score: _____/18

Next Activity (Next Day)
Study Cards (in Student Edition) & Speed Builder #4, p. 42

Here's your hint.

↓

$1 \times 1 = 1$
$2 \times 2 = 4$
$3 \times 3 = 9$
$4 \times 4 = 16$
$5 \times 5 = 25$
NEW⟩ $6 \times 6 =$ 36 six, six, thirty-six (a rhyme)
NEW⟩ $7 \times 7 =$ 49 Sevens Twins forgot a star
NEW⟩ $8 \times 8 =$ 64 Nintendo 64
$9 \times 9 = 81$

Use the mnemonic devices to the left to memorize the Squares. Flip the page and keep working.

Do not write any other hints on this page.

As you rehearse, the facts will move from your short-term memory into your long-term memory.

The Big Bad Numbers

Magic Sequence Navigator

10 Powerful Steps to Multiplication Fluency

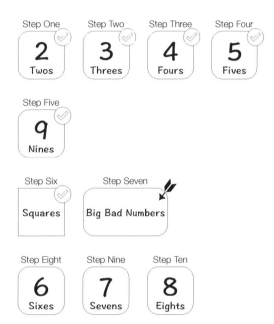

Step One
2
Twos ✓

Step Two
3
Threes ✓

Step Three
4
Fours ✓

Step Four
5
Fives ✓

Step Five
9
Nines ✓

Step Six
Squares ✓

Step Seven
Big Bad Numbers

Step Eight
6
Sixes

Step Nine
7
Sevens

Step Ten
8
Eights

Action Plan & Success Tracker

Complete each activity in the order shown below. ✓

A. **Speed Builder #1** (Pre-Test) page 48	
B. **Memory Builder** page 49	
C. Study Cards & **Speed Builder #2** page 48	
D. Study Cards & **Speed Builder #3** page 48	
E. Study Cards & **Distributed Practice** (at home) page 51	
Speed Builder #4: Wait until the next day.	
F. Study Cards & **Speed Builder #4** (Final) page 48	

Take a break now.

TEACHERS: If using a two-day pacing, assign the Extra **Memory Builder** here, before starting Activity D. The Extra Memory Builder is found in the teacher edition on page 93.

Big Bad Numbers

Speed Builders: Big Bad Numbers

Name_____

Goal: Show improvement after each Speed Builder. Score 100% correct by Speed Builder #4 (next day).
Target Time: One minute per column. Adjust time only if necessary.
Directions: Go in order, and do not skip around. If you don't recall a fact within two seconds, move on to the next problem.

Speed Builder #1
Pre-Test

6 x 6	=	
6 x 7	=	
6 x 8	=	
6 x 9	=	
7 x 7	=	
7 x 8	=	
7 x 9	=	
8 x 8	=	
8 x 9	=	
9 x 9	=	
6 x 6	=	
6 x 8	=	
7 x 7	=	
7 x 9	=	
8 x 9	=	
6 x 7	=	
6 x 9	=	
7 x 8	=	
8 x 8	=	
9 x 9	=	
6 x 7	=	
6 x 9	=	
7 x 8	=	
7 x 9	=	
8 x 9	=	
9 x 9	=	
8 x 9	=	
8 x 8	=	
7 x 9	=	
7 x 8	=	
7 x 7	=	
6 x 9	=	
6 x 8	=	
6 x 7	=	
6 x 6	=	

Pre-Test Score:_____/35

NEXT: Memory Builder & Study Cards

FOLD along dotted line to hide previous answers.

Speed Builder #2
Practice

6 x 6	=	
7 x 6	=	
8 x 6	=	
9 x 6	=	
7 x 7	=	
8 x 7	=	
9 x 7	=	
8 x 8	=	
9 x 8	=	
9 x 9	=	
6 x 6	=	
8 x 6	=	
7 x 7	=	
9 x 7	=	
9 x 8	=	
7 x 6	=	
9 x 6	=	
8 x 7	=	
8 x 8	=	
9 x 9	=	
7 x 6	=	
9 x 6	=	
8 x 7	=	
9 x 7	=	
9 x 8	=	
9 x 9	=	
9 x 8	=	
8 x 6	=	
9 x 7	=	
8 x 7	=	
7 x 7	=	
9 x 6	=	
8 x 6	=	
7 x 6	=	
6 x 6	=	

Practice Score: _____/35

NEXT AFTER (BREAK): Extra Memory Builder (if using two-day pacing) & Study Cards

FOLD along dotted line to hide previous answers.

Speed Builder #3
Practice

6 x 6	=	
6 x 7	=	
6 x 8	=	
6 x 9	=	
7 x 7	=	
7 x 8	=	
7 x 9	=	
8 x 8	=	
8 x 9	=	
9 x 9	=	
6 x 6	=	
6 x 8	=	
7 x 7	=	
7 x 9	=	
8 x 9	=	
6 x 7	=	
6 x 9	=	
7 x 8	=	
8 x 8	=	
9 x 9	=	
6 x 7	=	
6 x 9	=	
7 x 8	=	
7 x 9	=	
8 x 9	=	
9 x 9	=	
8 x 9	=	
8 x 8	=	
7 x 9	=	
7 x 8	=	
7 x 7	=	
6 x 9	=	
6 x 8	=	
6 x 7	=	
6 x 6	=	

Practice Score: _____/35

NEXT: Distributed Practice (at home) & Study Cards

FOLD along dotted line to hide previous answers.

Speed Builder #4
FINAL (taken the next day)

6 x 6	=	
7 x 6	=	
8 x 6	=	
9 x 6	=	
7 x 7	=	
8 x 7	=	
9 x 7	=	
8 x 8	=	
9 x 8	=	
9 x 9	=	
6 x 6	=	
8 x 6	=	
7 x 7	=	
9 x 7	=	
9 x 8	=	
7 x 6	=	
9 x 6	=	
8 x 7	=	
8 x 8	=	
9 x 9	=	
7 x 6	=	
9 x 6	=	
8 x 7	=	
9 x 7	=	
9 x 8	=	
9 x 9	=	
9 x 8	=	
8 x 6	=	
9 x 7	=	
8 x 7	=	
7 x 7	=	
9 x 6	=	
8 x 6	=	
7 x 6	=	
6 x 6	=	

FINAL Score: _____/35

Memory Builders: Big Bad Numbers

Big Bad Numbers

Name_____

Directions: Complete each row in order from left to right. *Do not skip around.*

Focus Facts: Row 1: ⑥ x ⑦
Row 2: ⑦ x ⑧
Row 3: ⑥ x ⑧

Two-Second Clock: `00:00:02`
If you don't recall a fact within two seconds, *flip the page for a hint.*

Cover up your Speed Builder results. Do not use any other hints, including multiplication tables, calculators, finger counting, tally marks, Refresher Posters, etc.

Magic Triangle

Row 1 Focus Facts: ⑥ x ⑦

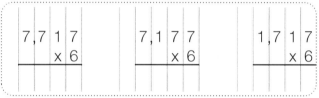

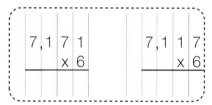

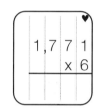

3-2-1 Memory Building System – First *three* problems: OK to flip the page for a hint.

Next *two* problems: Try not to flip the page.

Last *one*: Know facts by heart.

Row 2 Focus Facts: ⑦ x ⑧

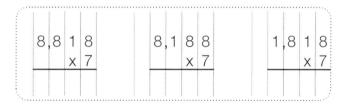

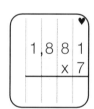

Row 3 Focus Facts: ⑥ x ⑧

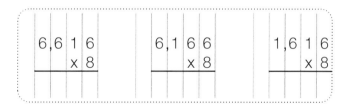

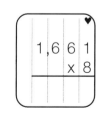

STUDENTS: Be sure to correct all mistakes.

Final Score: _____/18

Next Activity
Study Cards (in Student Edition)
& Speed Builder #2, p. 48

Here's your hint.

Magic Triangle

6 x 7	**#42 James Worthy** was once 6 feet, 7 inches tall
6 x 8	**six, eight, forty-eight** a rhyme
7 x 8	**5, 6, 7, 8** 56 = 7 x 8 The answer is also on a telephone keypad.

Make sure this page is hidden/covered and not easily seen when working on the **Memory Builders** and **Distributed Practice.**

Use the Magic Triangle and the mnemonic devices to the left to memorize the Big Bad Numbers. Flip the page and keep working.

Do not write any other hints on this page.

As you rehearse, the facts will move from your short-term memory into your long-term memory.

Big Bad Numbers

Distributed Practice: Big Bad Numbers

Distributed Practice (opposite of cramming) means spacing your practice sessions out over time in order to improve learning.

Name_____

Directions: Complete each row in order from left to right. ***Do not skip around.***

Two-Second Clock: `00:00:02`
If you don't recall a fact within two seconds, ***flip the page for a hint.***

Remember to cover up the hint page from the Memory Builder. Do not use multiplication tables, calculators, finger counting, tally marks, Refresher Posters, etc.

Focus Facts: Row 1: ⑥ x ⑦
Row 2: ⑦ x ⑧
Row 3: ⑥ x ⑧

Magic Triangle

Row 1 Focus Facts: ⑥ x ⑦

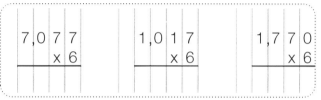

3-2-1 Memory Building System – First ***three*** problems: OK to flip the page for a hint.

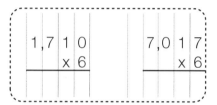

Next ***two*** problems: Try not to flip the page.

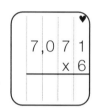

Last ***one***: Know facts by heart.

Row 2 Focus Facts: ⑦ x ⑧

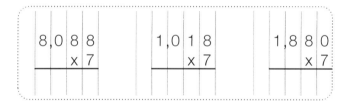

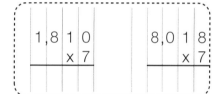

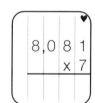

Row 3 Focus Facts: ⑥ x ⑧

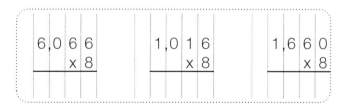

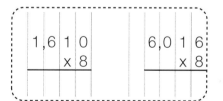

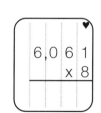

STUDENTS: Be sure to correct all mistakes.

Final Score: _____/18

Next Activity (Next Day)
Study Cards (in Student Edition) & Speed Builder#4, p. 48

Big Bad Numbers

Here's your hint.

Magic Triangle

Make sure this page is hidden/covered and not easily seen when working on the *Memory Builders* and *Distributed Practice.*

6 x 7	**#42 James Worthy** was once 6 feet, 7 inches tall
6 x 8	**six, eight, forty-eight** a rhyme
7 x 8	**5, 6, 7, 8** 56 = 7 x 8 The answer is also on a telephone keypad.

Use the Magic Triangle and the mnemonic devices to the left to memorize the Big Bad Numbers. Flip the page and keep working.

Do not write any other hints on this page.

As you rehearse, the facts will move from your short-term memory into your long-term memory.

Magic Sequence Navigator

10 Powerful Steps to Multiplication Fluency

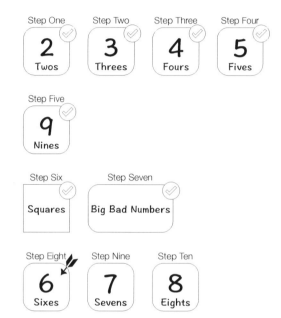

Step One — **2** Twos ✓
Step Two — **3** Threes ✓
Step Three — **4** Fours ✓
Step Four — **5** Fives ✓

Step Five — **9** Nines ✓

Step Six — Squares ✓
Step Seven — Big Bad Numbers ✓

Step Eight — **6** Sixes
Step Nine — **7** Sevens
Step Ten — **8** Eights

Action Plan & Success Tracker

Complete each activity in the order shown below.   ✓

A. **Speed Builder #1** (Pre-Test) page 54	
B. **Memory Builder** page 55	
C. Study Cards & **Speed Builder #2** *Take a break now.* page 54	
D. Study Cards & **Speed Builder #3** page 54	
E. Study Cards & **Distributed Practice** (at home) page 57	
Speed Builder #4: Wait until the next day.	
F. Study Cards & **Speed Builder #4** (Final) page 54	

TEACHERS: If using a two-day pacing, assign the Extra **Memory Builder** here, before starting Activity D. The Extra Memory Builder is found in the teacher edition on page 95.

Speed Builders: Sixes

Goal: Show improvement after each Speed Builder. Score 100% correct by Speed Builder #4 (next day).
Target Time: One minute per column. Adjust time only if necessary.
Directions: Go in order, and do not skip around. If you don't recall a fact within two seconds, move on to the next problem.

Name_____

Speed Builder #1
Pre-Test

2 x 6 = _____
5 x 6 = _____
7 x 6 = _____
9 x 6 = _____
6 x 6 = _____

5 x 6 = _____
9 x 6 = _____
2 x 6 = _____
7 x 6 = _____
4 x 6 = _____

6 x 6 = _____
3 x 6 = _____
8 x 6 = _____
5 x 6 = _____
9 x 6 = _____

3 x 6 = _____
2 x 6 = _____
8 x 6 = _____
4 x 6 = _____
7 x 6 = _____

6 x 6 = _____
8 x 6 = _____
3 x 6 = _____
4 x 6 = _____
7 x 6 = _____

3 x 6 = _____
2 x 6 = _____
5 x 6 = _____
4 x 6 = _____
6 x 6 = _____

9 x 6 = _____
8 x 6 = _____
6 x 6 = _____
3 x 6 = _____
2 x 6 = _____

Pre-Test Score:_____/35

NEXT: Memory Builder & Study Cards
FOLD along dotted line to hide previous answers.

Speed Builder #2
Practice

6 x 2 = _____
6 x 5 = _____
6 x 7 = _____
6 x 9 = _____
6 x 6 = _____

6 x 5 = _____
6 x 9 = _____
6 x 2 = _____
6 x 7 = _____
6 x 4 = _____

6 x 6 = _____
6 x 3 = _____
6 x 8 = _____
6 x 5 = _____
6 x 9 = _____

6 x 3 = _____
6 x 2 = _____
6 x 8 = _____
6 x 4 = _____
6 x 7 = _____

6 x 6 = _____
6 x 8 = _____
6 x 3 = _____
6 x 4 = _____
6 x 7 = _____

6 x 3 = _____
6 x 2 = _____
6 x 4 = _____
6 x 6 = _____

6 x 9 = _____
6 x 8 = _____
6 x 6 = _____
6 x 3 = _____
6 x 2 = _____

Practice Score: _____/35

NEXT AFTER (BREAK): Extra Memory Builder (if using two-day pacing) & Study Cards
FOLD along dotted line to hide previous answers.

Speed Builder #3
Practice

2 x 6 = _____
5 x 6 = _____
7 x 6 = _____
9 x 6 = _____
6 x 6 = _____

5 x 6 = _____
9 x 6 = _____
2 x 6 = _____
7 x 6 = _____
4 x 6 = _____

6 x 6 = _____
3 x 6 = _____
8 x 6 = _____
5 x 6 = _____
9 x 6 = _____

3 x 6 = _____
2 x 6 = _____
8 x 6 = _____
4 x 6 = _____
7 x 6 = _____

6 x 6 = _____
8 x 6 = _____
3 x 6 = _____
4 x 6 = _____
7 x 6 = _____

3 x 6 = _____
2 x 6 = _____
5 x 6 = _____
4 x 6 = _____
6 x 6 = _____

9 x 6 = _____
8 x 6 = _____
6 x 6 = _____
3 x 6 = _____
2 x 6 = _____

Practice Score: _____/35

NEXT: Distributed Practice (at home) & Study Cards
FOLD along dotted line to hide previous answers.

Speed Builder #4
FINAL (taken the next day)

6 x 2 = _____
6 x 5 = _____
6 x 7 = _____
6 x 9 = _____
6 x 6 = _____

6 x 5 = _____
6 x 9 = _____
6 x 2 = _____
6 x 7 = _____
6 x 4 = _____

6 x 6 = _____
6 x 3 = _____
6 x 8 = _____
6 x 5 = _____
6 x 9 = _____

6 x 3 = _____
6 x 2 = _____
6 x 8 = _____
6 x 4 = _____
6 x 7 = _____

6 x 6 = _____
6 x 8 = _____
6 x 3 = _____
6 x 4 = _____
6 x 7 = _____

6 x 3 = _____
6 x 2 = _____
6 x 5 = _____
6 x 4 = _____
6 x 6 = _____

6 x 9 = _____
6 x 8 = _____
6 x 6 = _____
6 x 3 = _____
6 x 2 = _____

FINAL Score: _____/35

Memory Builder: Sixes

Directions: Complete each row in order from left to right. ***Do not skip around.***

Focus Facts: Row 1: the digits ①, ④, and ⑦ multiplied by 6
Row 2: the digits ②, ⑤, and ⑧ multiplied by 6
Row 3: the digits ③, ⑥, and ⑨ multiplied by 6

Two-Second Clock: `00:00:02`
If you don't recall a fact within two seconds, ***flip the page for a hint.***

Cover up your Speed Builder results. Do not use any other hints, including multiplication tables, calculators, finger counting, tally marks, Refresher Posters, etc.

Row 1 Focus Facts: the digits ①, ④, and ⑦ multiplied by 6

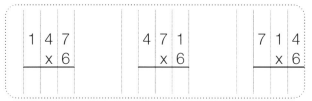

3-2-1 Memory Building System – First **three** problems: OK to flip the page for a hint.

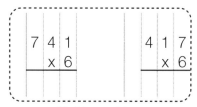

Next **two** problems: Try not to flip the page.

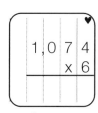

Last **one:** Know facts by heart.

Row 2 Focus Facts: the digits ②, ⑤, and ⑧ multiplied by 6

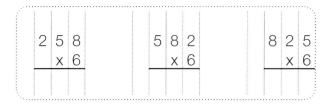

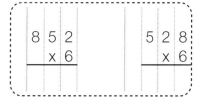

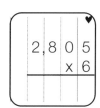

Row 3 Focus Facts: the digits ③, ⑥, and ⑨ multiplied by 6

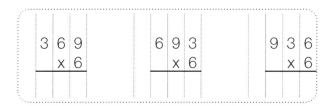

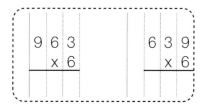

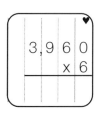

STUDENTS: Be sure to correct all mistakes.

Final Score: _____/18

Next Activity
Study Cards (in Student Edition)
& Speed Builder #2, p. 54

6

Sixes

**Here's
your hint.**

Multiples
of six

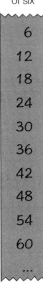

6

12

18

24

30

36

42

48

54

60

...

Make sure this page is hidden/covered and not easily seen when working on the *Memory Builders* and *Distributed Practice.*

With your pencil, touch the multiples of six in the correct order from top to bottom while saying,

> *"One time,"*
> *"two times,"*
> *"three times,"*

and so on until you reach the multiple that you're looking for.

Memorize it, flip the page over, and continue working.

Do not write any other hints on this page.

As you rehearse, the facts will move from your short-term memory into your long-term memory.

6
Sixes

Distributed Practice: Sixes

Distributed Practice means spacing your practice sessions out over time in order to improve learning. It is the opposite of cramming.

Name_____

Directions: Complete each row in order from left to right. **Do not skip around.**

Two-Second Clock: `00:00:02`
If you don't recall a fact within two seconds, **flip the page for a hint.**

Remember to cover up the hint page from the Memory Builder. Do not use multiplication tables, calculators, finger counting, tally marks, Refresher Posters, etc.

Focus Facts: Row 1: the digits ⑨, ⑥, and ① multiplied by 6
Row 2: the digits ⑧, ⑤, and ③ multiplied by 6
Row 3: the digits ⑦, ④, and ② multiplied by 6

Row 1 Focus Facts: the digits ⑨, ⑥, and ① multiplied by 6

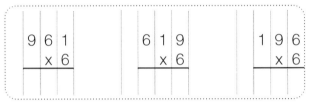

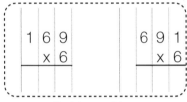

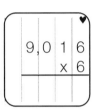

3-2-1 Memory Building System – First **three** problems:
OK to flip the page for a hint.

Next **two** problems:
Try not to flip the page.

Last **one:**
Know facts by heart.

Row 2 Focus Facts: the digits ⑧, ⑤, and ③ multiplied by 6

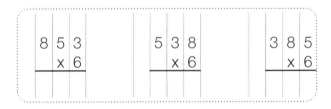

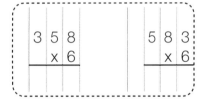

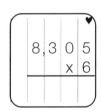

Row 3 Focus Facts: the digits ⑦, ④, and ② multiplied by 6

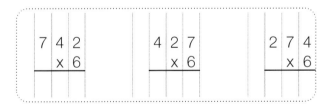

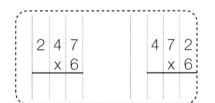

STUDENTS: Be sure to correct all mistakes.

Final Score: _____ /18

Next Activity (Next Day)
Study Cards (in Student Edition)
& Speed Builder #4, p. 54

**Here's
your hint.**

Multiples
of six

6
12
18
24
30
36
42
48
54
60
...

Make sure this page is hidden/covered and not easily seen when working on the **Memory Builders** and **Distributed Practice.**

With your pencil, touch the multiples of six in the correct order from top to bottom while saying,

"One time,"
"two times,"
"three times,"

and so on until you reach the multiple that you're looking for.

Memorize it, flip the page over, and continue working.

Do not write any other hints on this page.

As you rehearse, the facts will move from your short-term memory into your long-term memory.

Reveal the Pattern: Sixes

The multiples of six have created a secret hidden pattern in the Hundred Chart below. Reveal the pattern by *counting by six* and shading in the correct boxes. The first one has been done for you.

1	2	3	4	5	6	7	8	9	10
11	12	13	14	15	16	17	18	19	20
21	22	23	24	25	26	27	28	29	30
31	32	33	34	35	36	37	38	39	40
41	42	43	44	45	46	47	48	49	50
51	52	53	54	55	56	57	58	59	60
61	62	63	64	65	66	67	68	69	70
71	72	73	74	75	76	77	78	79	80
81	82	83	84	85	86	87	88	89	90
91	92	93	94	95	96	97	98	99	100

The Sevens

Magic Sequence Navigator

10 Powerful Steps to Multiplication Fluency

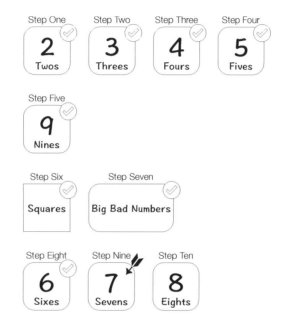

Step One	Step Two	Step Three	Step Four
2 Twos ✓	**3** Threes ✓	**4** Fours ✓	**5** Fives ✓

Step Five — **9** Nines ✓

Step Six — Squares ✓

Step Seven — Big Bad Numbers ✓

Step Eight	Step Nine	Step Ten
6 Sixes ✓	**7** Sevens	**8** Eights

Action Plan & Success Tracker

Complete each activity in the order shown below. ✓

A. **Speed Builder #1** (Pre-Test)	page 60
B. **Memory Builder**	page 61
C. Study Cards & **Speed Builder #2**	page 60
Take a break now.	
D. Study Cards & **Speed Builder #3**	page 60
E. Study Cards & **Distributed Practice** (at home)	page 63
Speed Builder #4: Wait until the next day.	
F. Study Cards & **Speed Builder #4** (Final)	page 60

TEACHERS: If using a two-day pacing, assign the Extra **Memory Builder** here, before starting Activity D. The Extra Memory Builder is found in the teacher edition on page 97.

Speed Builders: Sevens

Name_____

Goal: Show improvement after each Speed Builder. Score 100% correct by Speed Builder #4 (next day).
Target Time: One minute per column. Adjust time only if necessary.
Directions: Go in order, and do not skip around. If you don't recall a fact within two seconds, move on to the next problem.

Speed Builder #1
Pre-Test

2 x 7 = _____
5 x 7 = _____
7 x 7 = _____
9 x 7 = _____
6 x 7 = _____

5 x 7 = _____
9 x 7 = _____
2 x 7 = _____
7 x 7 = _____
4 x 7 = _____

6 x 7 = _____
3 x 7 = _____
8 x 7 = _____
5 x 7 = _____
9 x 7 = _____

3 x 7 = _____
2 x 7 = _____
8 x 7 = _____
4 x 7 = _____
7 x 7 = _____

6 x 7 = _____
8 x 7 = _____
3 x 7 = _____
4 x 7 = _____
7 x 7 = _____

3 x 7 = _____
2 x 7 = _____
5 x 7 = _____
4 x 7 = _____
6 x 7 = _____

9 x 7 = _____
8 x 7 = _____
6 x 7 = _____
3 x 7 = _____
2 x 7 = _____

Pre-Test Score:_____/35

NEXT: Memory Builder & Study Cards ------

FOLD along dotted line to hide previous answers.

Speed Builder #2
Practice

7 x 2 = _____
7 x 5 = _____
7 x 7 = _____
7 x 9 = _____
7 x 6 = _____

7 x 5 = _____
7 x 9 = _____
7 x 2 = _____
7 x 7 = _____
7 x 4 = _____

7 x 6 = _____
7 x 3 = _____
7 x 8 = _____
7 x 5 = _____
7 x 9 = _____

7 x 3 = _____
7 x 2 = _____
7 x 8 = _____
7 x 4 = _____
7 x 7 = _____

7 x 6 = _____
7 x 8 = _____
7 x 3 = _____
7 x 4 = _____
7 x 7 = _____

7 x 3 = _____
7 x 2 = _____
7 x 5 = _____
7 x 4 = _____
7 x 6 = _____

7 x 9 = _____
7 x 8 = _____
7 x 6 = _____
7 x 3 = _____
7 x 2 = _____

Practice Score: _____/35

NEXT AFTER (BREAK): Extra Memory Builder (if using two-day pacing) & Study Cards ------

FOLD along dotted line to hide previous answers.

Speed Builder #3
Practice

2 x 7 = _____
5 x 7 = _____
7 x 7 = _____
9 x 7 = _____
6 x 7 = _____

5 x 7 = _____
9 x 7 = _____
2 x 7 = _____
7 x 7 = _____
4 x 7 = _____

6 x 7 = _____
3 x 7 = _____
8 x 7 = _____
5 x 7 = _____
9 x 7 = _____

3 x 7 = _____
2 x 7 = _____
8 x 7 = _____
4 x 7 = _____
7 x 7 = _____

6 x 7 = _____
8 x 7 = _____
3 x 7 = _____
4 x 7 = _____
7 x 7 = _____

3 x 7 = _____
2 x 7 = _____
5 x 7 = _____
4 x 7 = _____
6 x 7 = _____

9 x 7 = _____
8 x 7 = _____
6 x 7 = _____
3 x 7 = _____
2 x 7 = _____

Practice Score: _____/35

NEXT: Distributed Practice (at home) & Study Cards ------

FOLD along dotted line to hide previous answers.

Speed Builder #4
FINAL (taken the next day)

7 x 2 = _____
7 x 5 = _____
7 x 7 = _____
7 x 9 = _____
7 x 6 = _____

7 x 5 = _____
7 x 9 = _____
7 x 2 = _____
7 x 7 = _____
7 x 4 = _____

7 x 6 = _____
7 x 3 = _____
7 x 8 = _____
7 x 5 = _____
7 x 9 = _____

7 x 3 = _____
7 x 2 = _____
7 x 8 = _____
7 x 4 = _____
7 x 7 = _____

7 x 6 = _____
7 x 8 = _____
7 x 3 = _____
7 x 4 = _____
7 x 7 = _____

7 x 3 = _____
7 x 2 = _____
7 x 5 = _____
7 x 4 = _____
7 x 6 = _____

7 x 9 = _____
7 x 8 = _____
7 x 6 = _____
7 x 3 = _____
7 x 2 = _____

FINAL Score: _____/35

10 Powerful Steps to Multiplication Fluency | © MathFluency.com | **Teachers: Log in for demo videos.**

Memory Builder: Sevens

Directions: Complete each row in order from left to right. **Do not skip around.**

Focus Facts: Row 1: the digits ①, ④, and ⑦ multiplied by 7
Row 2: the digits ②, ⑤, and ⑧ multiplied by 7
Row 3: the digits ③, ⑥, and ⑨ multiplied by 7

Two-Second Clock: | 00:00:02 |
If you don't recall a fact within two seconds, **flip the page for a hint.**

Cover up your Speed Builder results. Do not use any other hints, including multiplication tables, calculators, finger counting, tally marks, Refresher Posters, etc.

Row 1 Focus Facts: the digits ①, ④, and ⑦ multiplied by 7

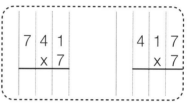

| 1 4 7 | 4 7 1 | 7 1 4 |
| x 7 | x 7 | x 7 |

3-2-1 Memory Building System – First **three** problems: OK to flip the page for a hint.

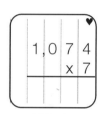

| 7 4 1 | 4 1 7 |
| x 7 | x 7 |

Next **two** problems: Try not to flip the page.

| 1,0 7 4 |
| x 7 |

Last **one:** Know facts by heart.

Row 2 Focus Facts: the digits ②, ⑤, and ⑧ multiplied by 7

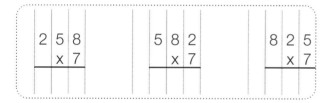

| 2 5 8 | 5 8 2 | 8 2 5 |
| x 7 | x 7 | x 7 |

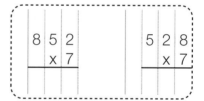

| 8 5 2 | 5 2 8 |
| x 7 | x 7 |

| 2,8 0 5 |
| x 7 |

Row 3 Focus Facts: the digits ③, ⑥, and ⑨ multiplied by 7

| 3 6 9 | 6 9 3 | 9 3 6 |
| x 7 | x 7 | x 7 |

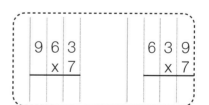

| 9 6 3 | 6 3 9 |
| x 7 | x 7 |

| 3,9 6 0 |
| x 7 |

STUDENTS: Be sure to correct all mistakes.

Final Score: _____/18

Next Activity
Study Cards (in Student Edition) & Speed Builder #2, p. 60

**Here's
your hint.**

Multiples
of seven

7
14
21
28
35
42
49
56
63
70
...

Make sure this page is hidden/covered and not easily seen when working on the **Memory Builders** and **Distributed Practice.**

With your pencil, touch the multiples of seven in the correct order from top to bottom while saying,

"One time,"
"two times,"
"three times,"

and so on until you reach the multiple that you're looking for.

Memorize it, flip the page over, and continue working.

Do not write any other hints on this page.

As you rehearse, the facts will move from your short-term memory into your long-term memory.

7 Sevens

Distributed Practice: Sevens

Name_____

Distributed Practice means spacing your practice sessions out over time in order to improve learning. It is the opposite of cramming.

Directions: Complete each row in order from left to right. ***Do not skip around.***

Two-Second Clock: `00:00:02`
If you don't recall a fact within two seconds, ***flip the page for a hint.***

Remember to cover up the hint page from the Memory Builder.
Do not use multiplication tables, calculators, finger counting, tally marks, Refresher Posters, etc.

Focus Facts: Row 1: the digits ⑨, ⑥, and ① multiplied by 7
Row 2: the digits ⑧, ⑤, and ③ multiplied by 7
Row 3: the digits ⑦, ④, and ② multiplied by 7

Row 1 Focus Facts: the digits ⑨, ⑥, and ① multiplied by 7

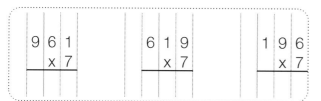

3-2-1 Memory Building System – First ***three*** problems:
OK to flip the page for a hint.

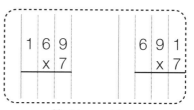

Next ***two*** problems:
Try not to flip the page.

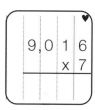

Last ***one:***
Know facts by heart.

Row 2 Focus Facts: the digits ⑧, ⑤, and ③ multiplied by 7

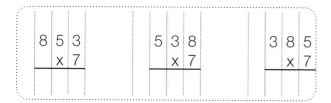

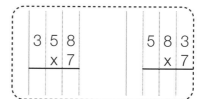

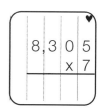

Row 3 Focus Facts: the digits ⑦, ④, and ② multiplied by 7

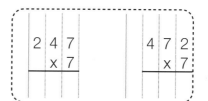

STUDENTS: Be sure to correct all mistakes.

Final Score: _____ /18

Next Activity (Next Day)
Study Cards (in Student Edition)
& Speed Builder #4, p. 60

7
Sevens

**Here's
your hint.**

↓

Multiples
of seven

| 7 |
| 14 |
| 21 |
| 28 |
| 35 |
| 42 |
| 49 |
| 56 |
| 63 |
| 70 |
| ... |

Make sure this page is hidden/covered and not easily seen when working on the *Memory Builders* and *Distributed Practice*.

With your pencil, touch the multiples of seven in the correct order from top to bottom while saying,

> *"One time,"*
> *"two times,"*
> *"three times,"*

and so on until you reach the multiple that you're looking for.

Memorize it, flip the page over, and continue working.

Do not write any other hints on this page.

As you rehearse, the facts will move from your short-term memory into your long-term memory.

Reveal the Pattern: Sevens

The multiples of seven have created a secret hidden pattern in the Hundred Chart below. Reveal the pattern by *counting by seven* and shading in the correct boxes. The first one has been done for you.

1	2	3	4	5	6	7	8	9	10
11	12	13	14	15	16	17	18	19	20
21	22	23	24	25	26	27	28	29	30
31	32	33	34	35	36	37	38	39	40
41	42	43	44	45	46	47	48	49	50
51	52	53	54	55	56	57	58	59	60
61	62	63	64	65	66	67	68	69	70
71	72	73	74	75	76	77	78	79	80
81	82	83	84	85	86	87	88	89	90
91	92	93	94	95	96	97	98	99	100

Step Ten
The Eights

Magic Sequence Navigator
10 Powerful Steps to Multiplication Fluency

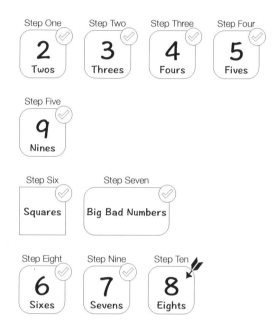

Step One
2 ✓
Twos

Step Two
3 ✓
Threes

Step Three
4 ✓
Fours

Step Four
5 ✓
Fives

Step Five
9 ✓
Nines

Step Six
✓
Squares

Step Seven
✓
Big Bad Numbers

Step Eight
6 ✓
Sixes

Step Nine
7 ✓
Sevens

Step Ten
8
Eights

Action Plan & Success Tracker
Complete each activity in the order shown below. ✓

A. **Speed Builder #1** (Pre-Test) page 66	
B. **Memory Builder** page 67	
C. Study Cards & **Speed Builder #2** page 66	
D. Study Cards & **Speed Builder #3** page 66	
E. Study Cards & **Distributed Practice** (at home) page 69	
Speed Builder #4: Wait until the next day.	
F. Study Cards & **Speed Builder #4** (Final) page 66	

Take a break now.

TEACHERS: If using a two-day pacing, assign the Extra **Memory Builder** here, before starting Activity D. The Extra Memory Builder is found in the teacher edition on page 99.

Step Ten

Speed Builders: Eights

Goal: Show improvement after each Speed Builder. Score 100% correct by Speed Builder #4 (next day).
Target Time: One minute per column. Adjust time only if necessary.
Directions: Go in order, and do not skip around. If you don't recall a fact within two seconds, move on to the next problem.

Speed Builder #1
Pre-Test

2 x 8 = _____
5 x 8 = _____
7 x 8 = _____
9 x 8 = _____
6 x 8 = _____

5 x 8 = _____
9 x 8 = _____
2 x 8 = _____
7 x 8 = _____
4 x 8 = _____

6 x 8 = _____
3 x 8 = _____
8 x 8 = _____
5 x 8 = _____
9 x 8 = _____

3 x 8 = _____
2 x 8 = _____
8 x 8 = _____
4 x 8 = _____
7 x 8 = _____

6 x 8 = _____
8 x 8 = _____
3 x 8 = _____
4 x 8 = _____
7 x 8 = _____

3 x 8 = _____
2 x 8 = _____
5 x 8 = _____
4 x 8 = _____
6 x 8 = _____

9 x 8 = _____
8 x 8 = _____
6 x 8 = _____
3 x 8 = _____
2 x 8 = _____

Pre-Test Score:_____/35

NEXT: Memory Builder & Study Cards

FOLD along dotted line to hide previous answers.

Speed Builder #2
Practice

8 x 2 = _____
8 x 5 = _____
8 x 7 = _____
8 x 9 = _____
8 x 6 = _____

8 x 5 = _____
8 x 9 = _____
8 x 2 = _____
8 x 7 = _____
8 x 4 = _____

8 x 6 = _____
8 x 3 = _____
8 x 8 = _____
8 x 5 = _____
8 x 9 = _____

8 x 3 = _____
8 x 2 = _____
8 x 8 = _____
8 x 4 = _____
8 x 7 = _____

8 x 6 = _____
8 x 8 = _____
8 x 3 = _____
8 x 4 = _____
8 x 7 = _____

8 x 3 = _____
8 x 2 = _____
8 x 5 = _____
8 x 4 = _____
8 x 6 = _____

8 x 9 = _____
8 x 8 = _____
8 x 6 = _____
8 x 3 = _____
8 x 2 = _____

Practice Score:_____/35

NEXT AFTER (BREAK): Extra Memory Builder (if using two-day pacing) & Study Cards

FOLD along dotted line to hide previous answers.

Speed Builder #3
Practice

2 x 8 = _____
5 x 8 = _____
7 x 8 = _____
9 x 8 = _____
6 x 8 = _____

5 x 8 = _____
9 x 8 = _____
2 x 8 = _____
7 x 8 = _____
4 x 8 = _____

6 x 8 = _____
3 x 8 = _____
8 x 8 = _____
5 x 8 = _____
9 x 8 = _____

3 x 8 = _____
2 x 8 = _____
8 x 8 = _____
4 x 8 = _____
7 x 8 = _____

6 x 8 = _____
8 x 8 = _____
3 x 8 = _____
4 x 8 = _____
6 x 8 = _____

9 x 8 = _____
8 x 8 = _____
6 x 8 = _____
3 x 8 = _____
2 x 8 = _____

Practice Score:_____/35

NEXT: Distributed Practice (at home) & Study Cards

FOLD along dotted line to hide previous answers.

Speed Builder #4
FINAL (taken the next day)

8 x 2 = _____
8 x 5 = _____
8 x 7 = _____
8 x 9 = _____
8 x 6 = _____

8 x 5 = _____
8 x 9 = _____
8 x 2 = _____
8 x 7 = _____
8 x 4 = _____

8 x 6 = _____
8 x 3 = _____
8 x 8 = _____
8 x 5 = _____
8 x 9 = _____

8 x 3 = _____
8 x 2 = _____
8 x 8 = _____
8 x 4 = _____
8 x 7 = _____

8 x 6 = _____
8 x 8 = _____
8 x 3 = _____
8 x 4 = _____
8 x 6 = _____

8 x 9 = _____
8 x 2 = _____
8 x 5 = _____
8 x 4 = _____
8 x 6 = _____

8 x 9 = _____
8 x 8 = _____
8 x 6 = _____
8 x 3 = _____
8 x 2 = _____

FINAL Score:_____/35

Memory Builder: Eights

Directions: Complete each row in order from left to right. **Do not skip around.**

Two-Second Clock: `00:00:02`
If you don't recall a fact within two seconds, **flip the page for a hint.**

Cover up your Speed Builder results. Do not use any other hints, including multiplication tables, calculators, finger counting, tally marks, Refresher Posters, etc.

Focus Facts: Row 1: the digits ①, ④, and ⑦ multiplied by 8
Row 2: the digits ②, ⑤, and ⑧ multiplied by 8
Row 3: the digits ③, ⑥, and ⑨ multiplied by 8

Row 1 Focus Facts: the digits ①, ④, and ⑦ multiplied by 8

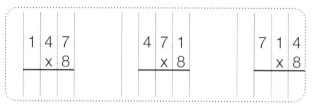

3-2-1 Memory Building System – First **three** problems: OK to flip the page for a hint.

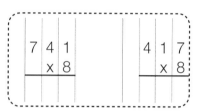

Next **two** problems: Try not to flip the page.

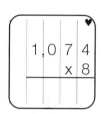

Last **one:** Know facts by heart.

Row 2 Focus Facts: the digits ②, ⑤, and ⑧ multiplied by 8

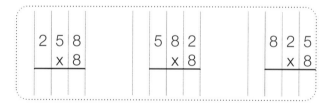

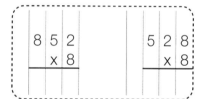

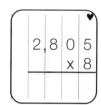

Row 3 Focus Facts: the digits ③, ⑥, and ⑨ multiplied by 8

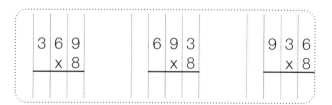

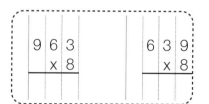

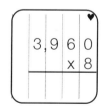

STUDENTS: Be sure to correct all mistakes.

Final Score: _____/18

Next Activity
Study Cards (in Student Edition) & Speed Builder #2, p. 66

**Here's
your hint.**

Multiples
of eight

8
16
24
32
40
48
56
64
72
80
...

Make sure this page is hidden/covered and not easily seen when working on the **Memory Builders** and **Distributed Practice.**

With your pencil, touch the multiples of eight in the correct order from top to bottom while saying,

> *"One time,"*
> *"two times,"*
> *"three times,"*

and so on until you reach the multiple that you're looking for.

Memorize it, flip the page over, and continue working.

Do not write any other hints on this page.

As you rehearse, the facts will move from your short-term memory into your long-term memory.

Step Ten

8 Eights

Distributed Practice: Eights

Distributed Practice means spacing your practice sessions out over time in order to improve learning. It is the opposite of cramming.

Name_____

Directions: Complete each row in order from left to right. **Do not skip around.**

Two-Second Clock: `00:00:02`
If you don't recall a fact within two seconds, **flip the page for a hint.**

Remember to cover up the hint page from the Memory Builder.
Do not use multiplication tables, calculators, finger counting, tally marks, Refresher Posters, etc.

Focus Facts: Row 1: the digits ⑨, ⑥, and ① multiplied by 8
Row 2: the digits ⑧, ⑤, and ③ multiplied by 8
Row 3: the digits ⑦, ④, and ② multiplied by 8

Row 1 Focus Facts: the digits ⑨, ⑥, and ① multiplied by 8

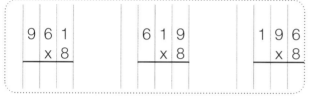

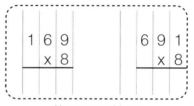

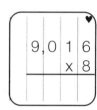

3-2-1 Memory Building System – First **three** problems: OK to flip the page for a hint.

Next **two** problems: Try not to flip the page.

Last **one:** Know facts by heart.

Row 2 Focus Facts: the digits ⑧, ⑤, and ③ multiplied by 8

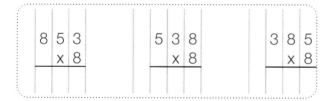

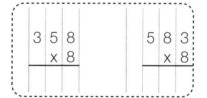

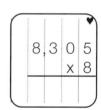

Row 3 Focus Facts: the digits ⑦, ④, and ② multiplied by 8

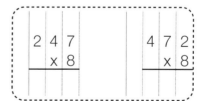

STUDENTS: Be sure to correct all mistakes.

Final Score: _____ /18

Next Activity (Next Day)
Study Cards (in Student Edition) & Speed Builder #4, p. 66

Eights

Here's your hint.

Multiples of eight

| 8 |
| 16 |
| 24 |
| 32 |
| 40 |
| 48 |
| 56 |
| 64 |
| 72 |
| 80 |
| ... |

Make sure this page is hidden/covered and not easily seen when working on the *Memory Builders* and *Distributed Practice*.

With your pencil, touch the multiples of eight in the correct order from top to bottom while saying,

> *"One time,"*
> *"two times,"*
> *"three times,"*

and so on until you reach the multiple that you're looking for.

Memorize it, flip the page over, and continue working.

Do not write any other hints on this page.

As you rehearse, the facts will move from your short-term memory into your long-term memory.

Reveal the Pattern: Eights

The multiples of eight have created a secret hidden pattern in the Hundred Chart below. Reveal the pattern by *counting by eight* and shading in the correct boxes. The first one has been done for you.

1	2	3	4	5	6	7	8	9	10
11	12	13	14	15	16	17	18	19	20
21	22	23	24	25	26	27	28	29	30
31	32	33	34	35	36	37	38	39	40
41	42	43	44	45	46	47	48	49	50
51	52	53	54	55	56	57	58	59	60
61	62	63	64	65	66	67	68	69	70
71	72	73	74	75	76	77	78	79	80
81	82	83	84	85	86	87	88	89	90
91	92	93	94	95	96	97	98	99	100

Appendix A and Appendix B

The ten steps of the Magic Sequence are designed to build multiplication fluency.

Appendix A and Appendix B are bookends that complement the system, and they are designed to build conceptual understanding. All the lessons in Appendix A and Appendix B are **guided lessons,** and students should complete them by following along with their instructor.

Appendix
A

Step One	Step Two	Step Three	Step Four	Step Five	Step Six	Step Seven	Step Eight	Step Nine	Step Ten
2 Twos	3 Threes	4 Fours	5 Fives	9 Nines	Squares	Big Bad Numbers	6 Sixes	7 Sevens	8 Eights

Appendix
B

pages 72-75

pages 76-78

Use Appendix A **before** using Step One.

Appendix A shows that multiplication is simply a shortcut for repeated addition.

Use Appendix B only **after** Step Ten.

Appendix B gives a Behind the Scenes look at multi-digit multiplication.

Appendix A-1: Multiplication is a Shortcut for Repeated Addition

Directions: Diagram each problem, and show how multiplication is just a short way of describing repeated addition.

A. There are three sea turtles. Each sea turtle has four legs. How many legs are there in all?

Repeated Addition: _____ + _____ + _____ = _____

Describe the repetition: _____ _____ ____

Multiplication: ____ ____ ____ = ____

B. There are four ladybugs. Each ladybug has six legs. How many legs are there in all?

Repeated Addition:

Describe the repetition:

Multiplication:

C. There are three spiders. Each spider has eight legs. How many legs are there in all?

Repeated Addition:

Describe the repetition:

Multiplication:

D. There are seven sea stars. Each sea star has five arms. How many arms are there in all?

Repeated Addition:

Multiplication:

Appendix A-2: Repeated Addition Using Arrays

Part 1: An array is an ordered arrangement using rows and columns. Show each array as a repeated addition problem and as a multiplication problem. (Note: It's conventional to list rows first, then columns. For example, a 2 x 5 array has 2 rows and 5 columns, and a 5 x 2 array has 5 rows and 2 columns.)

A. Put the eggs into equal groups **by row** (conventional). ____ ____ ____ Describe the repetition: _____ _____ ____ Multiplication:	B. Put the eggs into equal groups **by column.** ___ ___ ___ ___ Multiplication:
C. Put the eggs into equal groups **by row** (conventional). ____ ____ Multiplication:	D. Put the eggs into equal groups **by column.** ___ ___ ___ ___ ___ ___ Multiplication:

Part 2: Use the tick marks to draw each grid. Number each row and column, then write two multiplication facts.

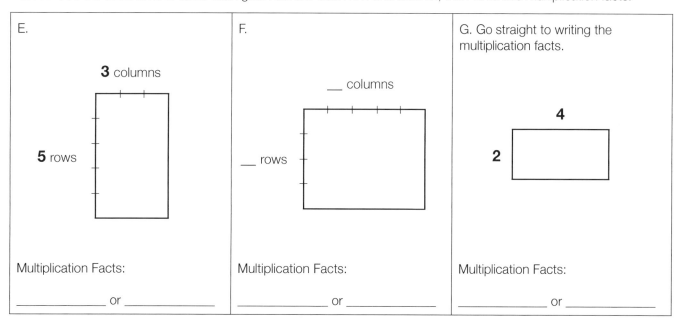

E.

3 columns

5 rows

Multiplication Facts:

_____ or _____

F.

__ columns

__ rows

Multiplication Facts:

_____ or _____

G. Go straight to writing the multiplication facts.

4

2

Multiplication Facts:

_____ or _____

Appendix A-3: Repeated Addition Using Number Lines

Directions: Label each number line to show how repeated addition is the same as multiplication.

A.

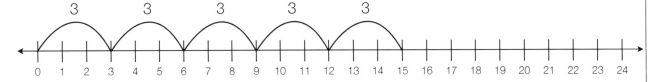

Repeated Addition: ____ + ____ + ____ + ____ + ____ = ____

Describe the repetition: _____ _____ ____

Multiplication: ____ ____ ____ = ____

B.

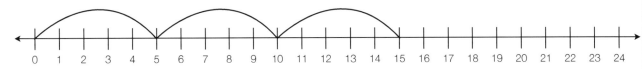

Repeated Addition:

Multiplication:

C.   3 + 3 + 3 + 3 + 3 + 3 + 3 + 3

Repeated Addition:

Multiplication:

D.   2 + 2 + 2 + 2 + 2 + 2 + 2 + 2 + 2

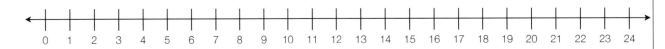

Repeated Addition:

Multiplication:

E.   53 + 53 + 53 + 53 + 53 + 53 + 53 + 53 + 53 + 53 + 53 + 53 + 53 +53 + 53 + 53 + 53 + 53 + 53

As the number of _____ increases, it becomes more and more _____ to use a number line to show repeated addition. Describe the repetition above, then write it as a multiplication problem instead.

Describe the repetition:

Multiplication (write only the expression without evaluating it):

Appendix A-4: Repeated Addition Using Skip Counting on a Hundred Chart

Part 1: Use the Hundred Charts to skip count. Lightly shade in the correct boxes to reveal a hidden pattern.

A. Skip count by 4. The first three are done for you.	B. Skip count by 9. (HINT: Eleven boxes should be shaded in).	C. Skip count by 2.

Hundred Chart (A)

1	2	3	4	5	6	7	8	9	10
11	12	13	14	15	16	17	18	19	20
21	22	23	24	25	26	27	28	29	30
31	32	33	34	35	36	37	38	39	40
41	42	43	44	45	46	47	48	49	50
51	52	53	54	55	56	57	58	59	60
61	62	63	64	65	66	67	68	69	70
71	72	73	74	75	76	77	78	79	80
81	82	83	84	85	86	87	88	89	90
91	92	93	94	95	96	97	98	99	100

Hundred Chart (B)

1	2	3	4	5	6	7	8	9	10
11	12	13	14	15	16	17	18	19	20
21	22	23	24	25	26	27	28	29	30
31	32	33	34	35	36	37	38	39	40
41	42	43	44	45	46	47	48	49	50
51	52	53	54	55	56	57	58	59	60
61	62	63	64	65	66	67	68	69	70
71	72	73	74	75	76	77	78	79	80
81	82	83	84	85	86	87	88	89	90
91	92	93	94	95	96	97	98	99	100

Hundred Chart (C)

1	2	3	4	5	6	7	8	9	10
11	12	13	14	15	16	17	18	19	20
21	22	23	24	25	26	27	28	29	30
31	32	33	34	35	36	37	38	39	40
41	42	43	44	45	46	47	48	49	50
51	52	53	54	55	56	57	58	59	60
61	62	63	64	65	66	67	68	69	70
71	72	73	74	75	76	77	78	79	80
81	82	83	84	85	86	87	88	89	90
91	92	93	94	95	96	97	98	99	100

List the first ten multiples of 4.

List the first ten multiples of 9.

List the first ten multiples of 2.

Part 2: Skip count to find the first ten multiples.

Skip count by 3.	Skip count by 5.	Skip count by 6.	Skip count by 7.	Skip count by 8.

Name_____

Appendix B-1: Behind the Scenes – Multi-digit by Single Digit Multiplication

Part 1: Distributive Property – Follow along with your instructor to complete this lesson.

A. Multiply.	B. Expand vertically.	C. Expand vertically, then multiply.
1 2 3 x 3	1 2 3	1 2 3 x 3

D. Decompose (break up) the array, then multiply. Use the arrows below and your answer from Box B to help you.

123

3

3(123) =

Note: As you practice and become fluent, you'll be able to do problems like this completely in your head!

Part 2: Distributive Property

E. Multiply.	F. Expand vertically.	G. Expand vertically, then multiply.
4 5 9 x 9	4 5 9	4 5 9 x 9

H. Draw an area model, then multiply.

9(459) =

Note: This one is harder to do in your head because it involves regrouping multiple times.

Name_____

Appendix B-2: Behind the Scenes – Multi-digit by Multi-digit Multiplication

Part 1: Distributive Property – Follow along with your instructor to complete this lesson.

A. Multiply. $\begin{array}{r} 2\,3 \\ \times\,2\,1 \\ \hline \end{array}$	B. Solve the problem to the left using **expanded notation.**

C. Decompose the array, then multiply.

21

23

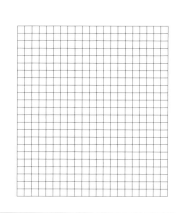

Part 2: Distributive Property

D. Multiply. $\begin{array}{r} 2\,4 \\ \times\,3\,2 \\ \hline \end{array}$	E. Solve the problem to the left using **expanded notation.**

F. Draw an area model, then multiply.

Name_____

Appendix B-3: Multiplying Multi-digit by Single-digit Numbers in Your Head

Part 1: Add. You should be able to do these problems in your head (add the tens, then add the ones).

A1.	A2.	B1.	B2.
420 + 10 + 8 = _____	120 + 16 = _____	350 + 20 + 1 = _____	360 + 24 = _____
560 + 10 + 4 = _____	360 + 12 = _____	360 + 20 + 4 = _____	560 + 28 = _____
120 + 10 + 6 = _____	420 + 18 = _____	560 + 20 + 8 = _____	630 + 27 = _____
360 + 10 + 2 = _____	560 + 14 = _____	630 + 20 + 7 = _____	350 + 21 = _____

Part 2: Follow along with your instructor to multiply from **LEFT to RIGHT** using **expanded notation.**

C. (Use Box A1. to help you.)	D.	E. (Use Box B1. to help you.)	F.
7 | 3 x | 6 Step i. **70** x 6 Step ii. 3 x 6 Step iii. Add.	8 | 2 x | 7 Step i. **80** x 7 Step ii. 2 x 7 Step iii. Add.	5 | 3 x | 7 Step i. **50** x 7 Step ii. 3 x 7 Step iii. Add.	9 | 6 x | 4 Step i. **90** x 4 Step ii. 6 x 4 Step iii. Add.

Part 3: Multiply in your head going from **LEFT to RIGHT.** Mentally use the same steps as in Parts 1 and 2.

G.	H.	I.	J.
3 | 4 x | 4	6 | 2 x | 6	7 | 3 x | 9	8 | 4 x | 7

Part 4: Add. You should be able to do these problems in your head.

K1.	K2.
200 + 60 + 10 + 2 = _____	600 + 210 + 12 = _____
600 + 200 + 10 + 10 + 2 = _____	1,200 + 60 + 9 = _____
800 + 100 + 60 + 10 + 2 = _____	200 + 60 + 12 = _____
1,000 + 200 + 60 + 9 = _____	800 + 160 + 12 = _____

Part 5: Follow along with your instructor to multiply from **LEFT to RIGHT** using **expanded notation.** Use Part 4 to help you. With plenty of practice, you will be able to do these types of problems completely in your head.

L. (Use Box K1. to help you.)	M.	N.	O.
1 | 3 | 6 x | | 2 Step i. **100** x 2 Step ii. 30 x 2 Step iii. 6 x 2 Step iv. Add.	4 | 2 | 3 x | | 3 Step i. **400** x 3 Step ii. 20 x 3 Step iii. 3 x 3 Step iv. Add.	2 | 7 | 4 x | | 3 Step i. **200** x 3 Step ii. 70 x 3 Step iii. 4 x 3 Step iv. Add.	4 | 8 | 6 x | | 2 Step i. **400** x 2 Step ii. 80 x 2 Step iii. 6 x 2 Step iv. Add.

Appendix C

Extra **Memory Builders**

Use these Extra **"Memory Builders"** to give students additional practice and support. The Memory Builders are especially important because they help students move their multiplication facts from short-term memory into long-term memory.

When breaking up the Action Plan into a two-day schedule (Pacing Option #2 on page 8), **assign an Extra "Memory Builder" before starting Activity D on the second day,** as shown below.

The Extra "Memory Builders" may also be used as refresher lessons. For example, after students have completed Steps 1-10, the teacher may review Steps 1-10 by assigning an Extra "Memory Builder" each day for ten days.

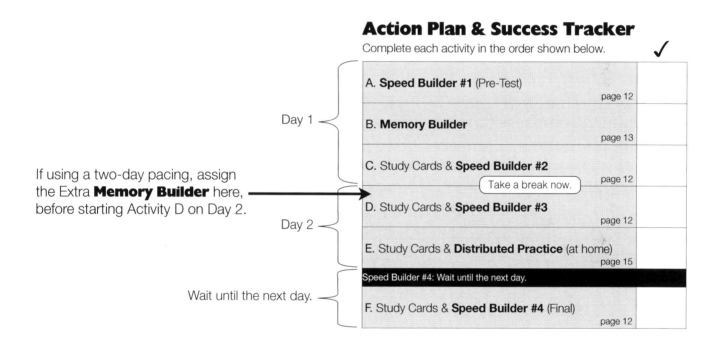

Action Plan & Success Tracker

Complete each activity in the order shown below. ✓

A. **Speed Builder #1** (Pre-Test) page 12	
B. **Memory Builder** page 13	
C. Study Cards & **Speed Builder #2** page 12	
D. Study Cards & **Speed Builder #3** page 12	
E. Study Cards & **Distributed Practice** (at home) page 15	
Speed Builder #4: Wait until the next day.	
F. Study Cards & **Speed Builder #4** (Final) page 12	

Day 1

Day 2

Take a break now.

If using a two-day pacing, assign the Extra **Memory Builder** here, before starting Activity D on Day 2.

Wait until the next day.

10 Powerful Steps to Multiplication Fluency | © MathFluency.com | **Teachers: Log in for demo videos.**

2 Twos | Extra **Memory Builder: Twos**

Name_____

Directions: Complete each row in order from left to right. **Do not skip around.**

Two-Second Clock: `00:00:02`
If you don't recall a fact within two seconds, **flip the page for a hint.**

Remember to cover up all other hints. Do not use multiplication tables, calculators, finger counting, tally marks, Refresher Posters, etc.

Focus Facts:
Row 1: the digits ⑤, ①, and ⑧ multiplied by 2
Row 2: the digits ④, ③, and ⑦ multiplied by 2
Row 3: the digits ⑥, ②, and ⑨ multiplied by 2

Row 1 Focus Facts: the digits ⑤, ①, and ⑧ multiplied by 2

```
 5 1 8      1 8 5      8 5 1
x  2      x   2      x   2
```
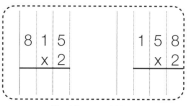
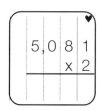

3-2-1 Memory Building System – First **three** problems: OK to flip the page for a hint.

Next **two** problems: Try not to flip the page.

Last **one:** Know facts by heart.

Row 2 Focus Facts: the digits ④, ③, and ⑦ multiplied by 2

```
 4 3 7      3 7 4      7 4 3
x  2      x   2      x   2
```
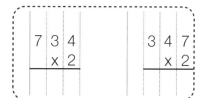

Row 3 Focus Facts: the digits ⑥, ②, and ⑨ multiplied by 2

```
 6 2 9      2 9 6      9 6 2
x  2      x   2      x   2
```
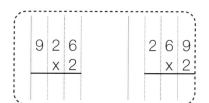
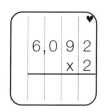

STUDENTS: Be sure to correct all mistakes.

Final Score: _____/18

Next Activity
Study Cards (in Student Edition)
& Speed Builder #3, p. 12

**Here's
your hint.**

Multiples
of two

2
4
6
8
10
12
14
16
18
20
...

Make sure this page is hidden/covered and not easily seen when working on the **Memory Builders** and **Distributed Practice.**

With your pencil, touch the multiples of two in the correct order from top to bottom while saying,

> *"One time,"*
> *"two times,"*
> *"three times,"*

and so on until you reach the multiple that you're looking for.

Memorize it, flip the page over, and continue working.

Do not write any other hints on this page.

As you rehearse, the facts will move from your short-term memory into your long-term memory.

3 Threes

Extra **Memory Builder: Threes**

Name_____

Directions: Complete each row in order from left to right. **Do not skip around.**

Two-Second Clock: `00:00:02`
If you don't recall a fact within two seconds, **flip the page for a hint.**

Remember to cover up all other hints. Do not use multiplication tables, calculators, finger counting, tally marks, Refresher Posters, etc.

Focus Facts:
Row 1: the digits ⑤, ①, and ⑧ multiplied by 3
Row 2: the digits ④, ③, and ⑦ multiplied by 3
Row 3: the digits ⑥, ②, and ⑨ multiplied by 3

Row 1 Focus Facts: the digits ⑤, ①, and ⑧ multiplied by 3

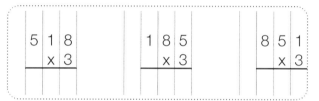

3-2-1 Memory Building System – First **three** problems:
OK to flip the page for a hint.

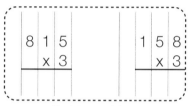

Next **two** problems:
Try not to flip the page.

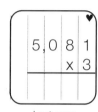

Last **one:**
Know facts by heart.

Row 2 Focus Facts: the digits ④, ③, and ⑦ multiplied by 3

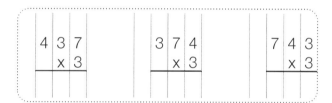

Row 3 Focus Facts: the digits ⑥, ②, and ⑨ multiplied by 3

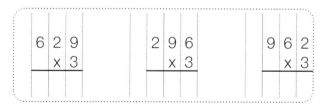

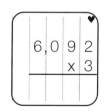

STUDENTS: Be sure to correct all mistakes.

Final Score: _____ /18

Next Activity
Study Cards (in Student Edition)
& Speed Builder #3, p. 18

**Here's
your hint.**

Multiples
of three

3
6
9
12
15
18
21
24
27
30
...

Make sure this page is hidden/covered and not easily seen when working on the *Memory Builders* and *Distributed Practice.*

With your pencil, touch the multiples of three in the correct order from top to bottom while saying,

> *"One time,"*
> *"two times,"*
> *"three times,"*

and so on until you reach the multiple that you're looking for.

Memorize it, flip the page over, and continue working.

Do not write any other hints on this page.

As you rehearse, the facts will move from your short-term memory into your long-term memory.

4 Fours

Extra **Memory Builder: Fours**

Name_____

Directions: Complete each row in order from left to right. ***Do not skip around.***

Two-Second Clock: `00:00:02`
If you don't recall a fact within two seconds, ***flip the page for a hint.***

Remember to cover up all other hints. Do not use multiplication tables, calculators, finger counting, tally marks, Refresher Posters, etc.

Focus Facts: Row 1: the digits ⑤, ①, and ⑧ multiplied by 4
Row 2: the digits ④, ③, and ⑦ multiplied by 4
Row 3: the digits ⑥, ②, and ⑨ multiplied by 4

Row 1 Focus Facts: the digits ⑤, ①, and ⑧ multiplied by 4

5 1 8 × 4	1 8 5 × 4	8 5 1 × 4

3-2-1 Memory Building System – First ***three*** problems: OK to flip the page for a hint.

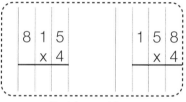

Next ***two*** problems: Try not to flip the page.

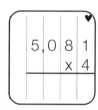

Last ***one:*** Know facts by heart.

Row 2 Focus Facts: the digits ④, ③, and ⑦ multiplied by 4

4 3 7 × 4	3 7 4 × 4	7 4 3 × 4

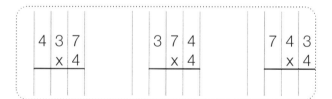

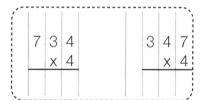

Row 3 Focus Facts: the digits ⑥, ②, and ⑨ multiplied by 4

6 2 9 × 4	2 9 6 × 4	9 6 2 × 4

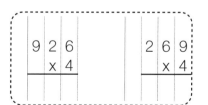

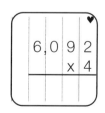

STUDENTS: Be sure to correct all mistakes.

Final Score: _____ /18

Next Activity
Study Cards (in Student Edition) & Speed Builder #3, p. 24

**Here's
your hint.**

Multiples
of four

4
8
12
16
20
24
28
32
36
40
...

Make sure this page is hidden/covered and not easily seen when working on the **Memory Builders** and **Distributed Practice.**

With your pencil, touch the multiples of four in the correct order from top to bottom while saying,

> *"One time,"*
> *"two times,"*
> *"three times,"*

and so on until you reach the multiple that you're looking for.

Memorize it, flip the page over, and continue working.

Do not write any other hints on this page.

As you rehearse, the facts will move from your short-term memory into your long-term memory.

Extra **Memory Builder: Fives**

Directions: Complete each row in order from left to right. **Do not skip around.**

Focus Facts: Row 1: the digits ⑤, ①, and ⑧ multiplied by 5
Row 2: the digits ④, ③, and ⑦ multiplied by 5
Row 3: the digits ⑥, ②, and ⑨ multiplied by 5

Two-Second Clock: 00:00:02

If you don't recall a fact within two seconds, **flip the page for a hint.**

Remember to cover up all other hints. Do not use multiplication tables, calculators, finger counting, tally marks, Refresher Posters, etc.

Row 1 Focus Facts: the digits ⑤, ①, and ⑧ multiplied by 5

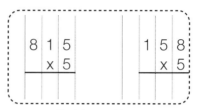 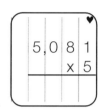

3-2-1 Memory Building System – First **three** problems: OK to flip the page for a hint.

Next **two** problems: Try not to flip the page.

Last **one:** Know facts by heart.

Row 2 Focus Facts: the digits ④, ③, and ⑦ multiplied by 5

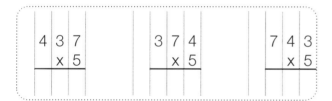 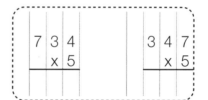 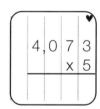

Row 3 Focus Facts: the digits ⑥, ②, and ⑨ multiplied by 5

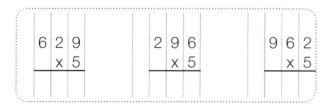 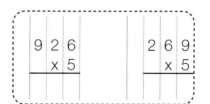 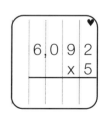

STUDENTS: Be sure to correct all mistakes.

Final Score: _____/18

Next Activity
Study Cards (in Student Edition)
& Speed Builder #3, p. 30

5

Fives

**Here's
your hint.**

Multiples
of five

5
10
15
20
25
30
35
40
45
50
...

Make sure this page is hidden/covered and not easily seen when working on the **Memory Builders** and **Distributed Practice.**

With your pencil, touch the multiples of five in the correct order from top to bottom while saying,

"One time,"
"two times,"
"three times,"

and so on until you reach the multiple that you're looking for.

Memorize it, flip the page over, and continue working.

Do not write any other hints on this page.

As you rehearse, the facts will move from your short-term memory into your long-term memory.

Step Five

9 Nines

Extra **Memory Builder: Nines**

Name_____

Directions: Complete each row in order from left to right. **Do not skip around.**

Two-Second Clock: `00:00:02`

If you don't recall a fact within two seconds, **flip the page for a hint.**

Remember to cover up all other hints. Do not use multiplication tables, calculators, finger counting, tally marks, Refresher Posters, etc.

Focus Facts: Row 1: the digits ⑤, ①, and ⑧ multiplied by 9
Row 2: the digits ④, ③, and ⑦ multiplied by 9
Row 3: the digits ⑥, ②, and ⑨ multiplied by 9

Magic Box

Row 1 Focus Facts: the digits ⑤, ①, and ⑧ multiplied by 9

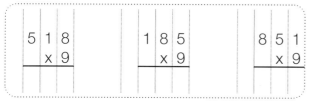

3-2-1 Memory Building System – First **three** problems: OK to flip the page for a hint.

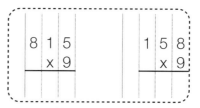

Next **two** problems: Try not to flip the page.

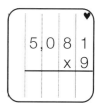

Last **one:** Know facts by heart.

Row 2 Focus Facts: the digits ④, ③, and ⑦ multiplied by 9

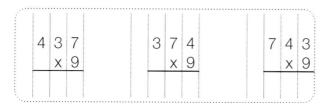

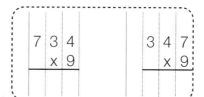

Row 3 Focus Facts: the digits ⑥, ②, and ⑨ multiplied by 9

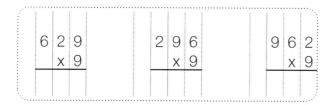

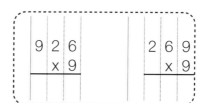

STUDENTS: Be sure to correct all mistakes.

Final Score: _____/18

Next Activity
Study Cards (in Student Edition)
& Speed Builder #3, p. 36

Step Five

9

Nines

**Here's
your hint.**

↓

Magic Box

1	2	3	4
8	7	6	5

↓ ↓ ↓ ↓
18 27 36 45
81 72 63 54

Make sure this page is hidden/covered and not easily seen when working on the *Memory Builders* and *Distributed Practice.*

When multiplying 9 by a single digit number from 2 to 9, "Think One Less," then use the Magic Box.

Example: 9 x 3 = ____

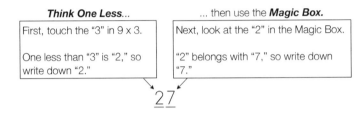

Think One Less...	*... then use the **Magic Box.***
First, touch the "3" in 9 x 3. One less than "3" is "2," so write down "2."	Next, look at the "2" in the Magic Box. "2" belongs with "7," so write down "7."

27

Answer: 9 x 3 = 27

Memorize it, flip the page over, and continue working.

Do not write any other hints on this page.

As you rehearse, the facts will move from your short-term memory into your long-term memory.

Name_____

Extra **Memory Builder: Squares**

Directions: Complete each row in order from left to right. ***Do not skip around.***

Two-Second Clock: `00:00:02`
If you don't recall a fact within two seconds, ***flip the page for a hint.***

Remember to cover up all other hints. Do not use multiplication tables, calculators, finger counting, tally marks, Refresher Posters, etc.

Focus Facts: Row 1: the digits ①, ④, and ⑦ squared
Row 2: the digits ②, ⑤, and ⑧ squared
Row 3: the digits ③, ⑥, and ⑨ squared

Row 1 Focus Facts: the digits ①, ④, and ⑦ squared

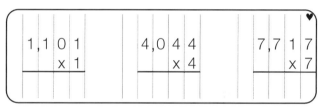

3-3 Memory Building System – First ***three*** problems:
OK to flip the page for a hint.

Last ***three*** problems:
Know the facts by heart.

Row 2 Focus Facts: the digits ②, ⑤, and ⑧ squared

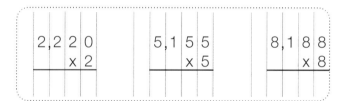

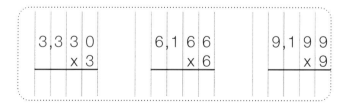

Row 3 Focus Facts: the digits ③, ⑥, and ⑨ squared

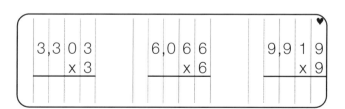

STUDENTS: Be sure to correct all mistakes.

Final Score: _____/18

Next Activity
Study Cards (in Student Edition)
& Speed Builder #3, p. 42

Step Six

Squares

Here's your hint.

↓

	1	x	1	=	1	
	2	x	2	=	4	
	3	x	3	=	9	
	4	x	4	=	16	
	5	x	5	=	25	
NEW	6	x	6	=	**36**	six, six, thirty-six (a rhyme)
NEW	7	x	7	=	**49**	Sevens Twins forgot a star
NEW	8	x	8	=	**64**	Nintendo 64
	9	x	9	=	81	

Make sure this page is hidden/covered and not easily seen when working on the ***Memory Builders*** and ***Distributed Practice.***

Use the mnemonic devices to the left to memorize the Squares. Flip the page and keep working.

Do not write any other hints on this page.

As you rehearse, the facts will move from your short-term memory into your long-term memory.

Name_____

Extra **Memory Builder: Big Bad Numbers**

Directions: Complete each row in order from left to right. **Do not skip around.**

Two-Second Clock: `00:00:02`

If you don't recall a fact within two seconds, **flip the page for a hint.**

Remember to cover up all other hints. Do not use multiplication tables, calculators, finger counting, tally marks, Refresher Posters, etc.

Focus Facts: Row 1: ⑥ x ⑦
Row 2: ⑦ x ⑧
Row 3: ⑥ x ⑧

Magic Triangle

Row 1 Focus Facts: ⑥ x ⑦

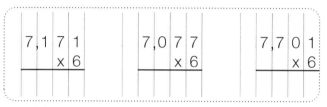

3-2-1 Memory Building System – First **three** problems:
OK to flip the page for a hint.

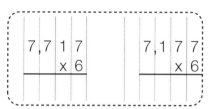

Next **two** problems:
Try not to flip the page.

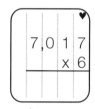

Last **one**:
Know facts by heart.

Row 2 Focus Facts: ⑦ x ⑧

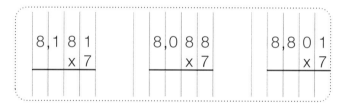

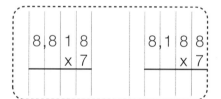

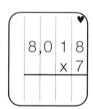

Row 3 Focus Facts: ⑥ x ⑧

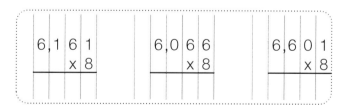

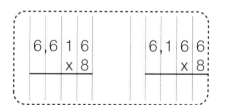

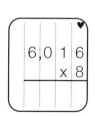

STUDENTS: Be sure to correct all mistakes.

Final Score: _____ /18

Next Activity
Study Cards (in Student Edition)
& Speed Builder #3, p. 48

Here's your hint.

Magic Triangle

6 x 7	**#42 James Worthy** was once 6 feet, 7 inches tall
6 x 8	**six, eight, forty-eight** a rhyme
7 x 8	**5, 6, 7, 8** 56 = 7 x 8 The answer is also on a telephone keypad.

Make sure this page is hidden/covered and not easily seen when working on the *Memory Builders* and *Distributed Practice.*

Use the Magic Triangle and the mnemonic devices to the left to memorize the Big Bad Numbers. Flip the page and keep working.

Do not write any other hints on this page.

As you rehearse, the facts will move from your short-term memory into your long-term memory.

6 Sixes

Extra **Memory Builder: Sixes**

Name_____

Directions: Complete each row in order from left to right. **Do not skip around.**

Two-Second Clock: `00:00:02`
If you don't recall a fact within two seconds, **flip the page for a hint.**

Remember to cover up all other hints. Do not use multiplication tables, calculators, finger counting, tally marks, Refresher Posters, etc.

Focus Facts: Row 1: the digits ⑤, ①, and ⑧ multiplied by 6
Row 2: the digits ④, ③, and ⑦ multiplied by 6
Row 3: the digits ⑥, ②, and ⑨ multiplied by 6

Row 1 Focus Facts: the digits ⑤, ①, and ⑧ multiplied by 6

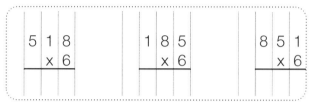

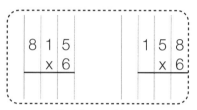

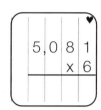

3-2-1 Memory Building System – First **three** problems: OK to flip the page for a hint.

Next **two** problems: Try not to flip the page.

Last **one:** Know facts by heart.

Row 2 Focus Facts: the digits ④, ③, and ⑦ multiplied by 6

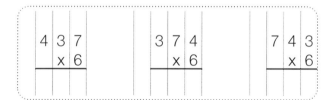

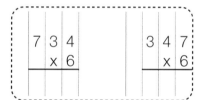

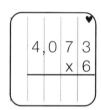

Row 3 Focus Facts: the digits ⑥, ②, and ⑨ multiplied by 6

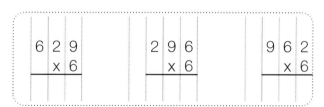

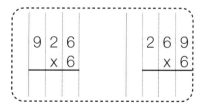

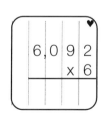

STUDENTS: Be sure to correct all mistakes.

Final Score: _____/18

Next Activity
Study Cards (in Student Edition)
& Speed Builder #3, p. 54

Step Eight

6
Sixes

**Here's
your hint.**

Multiples
of six

6
12
18
24
30
36
42
48
54
60
...

Make sure this page is hidden/covered and not easily seen when working on the *Memory Builders* and *Distributed Practice.*

With your pencil, touch the multiples of six in the correct order from top to bottom while saying,

> *"One time,"*
> *"two times,"*
> *"three times,"*

and so on until you reach the multiple that you're looking for.

Memorize it, flip the page over, and continue working.

Do not write any other hints on this page.

As you rehearse, the facts will move from your short-term memory into your long-term memory.

Extra **Memory Builder: Sevens**

Name_____

Directions: Complete each row in order from left to right. **Do not skip around.**

Focus Facts: Row 1: the digits ⑤, ①, and ⑧ multiplied by 7
Row 2: the digits ④, ③, and ⑦ multiplied by 7
Row 3: the digits ⑥, ②, and ⑨ multiplied by 7

Two-Second Clock: `00:00:02`
If you don't recall a fact within two seconds, **flip the page for a hint.**

Remember to cover up all other hints. Do not use multiplication tables, calculators, finger counting, tally marks, Refresher Posters, etc.

Row 1 Focus Facts: the digits ⑤, ①, and ⑧ multiplied by 7

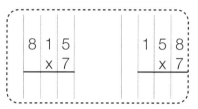

3-2-1 Memory Building System – First **three** problems:
OK to flip the page for a hint.

Next **two** problems:
Try not to flip the page.

Last **one:**
Know facts by heart.

Row 2 Focus Facts: the digits ④, ③, and ⑦ multiplied by 7

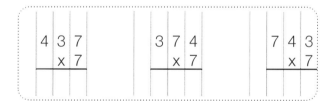

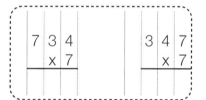

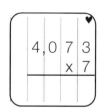

Row 3 Focus Facts: the digits ⑥, ②, and ⑨ multiplied by 7

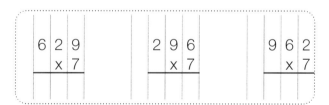

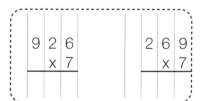

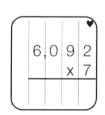

STUDENTS: Be sure to correct all mistakes.

Final Score: _____/18

Next Activity
Study Cards (in Student Edition)
& Speed Builder #3, p. 60

7

Sevens

Here's your hint.

Multiples of seven

7
14
21
28
35
42
49
56
63
70
...

Make sure this page is hidden/covered and not easily seen when working on the **Memory Builders** and **Distributed Practice.**

With your pencil, touch the multiples of seven in the correct order from top to bottom while saying,

"One time,"
"two times,"
"three times,"

and so on until you reach the multiple that you're looking for.

Memorize it, flip the page over, and continue working.

Do not write any other hints on this page.

As you rehearse, the facts will move from your short-term memory into your long-term memory.

Eights

Extra **Memory Builder: Eights**

Name_____

Directions: Complete each row in order from left to right. **Do not skip around.**

Focus Facts:
Row 1: the digits ⑤, ①, and ⑧ multiplied by 8
Row 2: the digits ④, ③, and ⑦ multiplied by 8
Row 3: the digits ⑥, ②, and ⑨ multiplied by 8

Two-Second Clock: `00:00:02`
If you don't recall a fact within two seconds, **flip the page for a hint.**

Remember to cover up all other hints. Do not use multiplication tables, calculators, finger counting, tally marks, Refresher Posters, etc.

Row 1 Focus Facts: the digits ⑤, ①, and ⑧ multiplied by 8

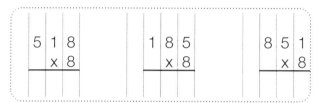
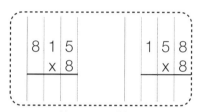
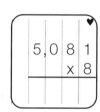

3-2-1 Memory Building System – First **three** problems: OK to flip the page for a hint.

Next **two** problems: Try not to flip the page.

Last **one:** Know facts by heart.

Row 2 Focus Facts: the digits ④, ③, and ⑦ multiplied by 8

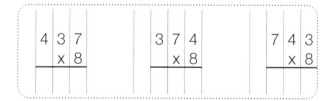
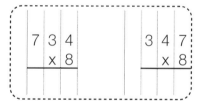
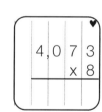

Row 3 Focus Facts: the digits ⑥, ②, and ⑨ multiplied by 8

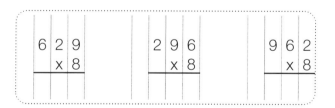
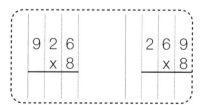
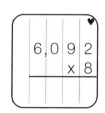

STUDENTS: Be sure to correct all mistakes.

Final Score: _____/18

Next Activity
Study Cards (in Student Edition) & Speed Builder #3, p. 66

8

Eights

**Here's
your hint.**

Multiples
of eight

8

16

24

32

40

48

56

64

72

80

...

Make sure this page is hidden/covered and not easily seen when working on the *Memory Builders* and *Distributed Practice.*

With your pencil, touch the multiples of eight in the correct order from top to bottom while saying,

"One time,"
"two times,"
"three times,"

and so on until you reach the multiple that you're looking for.

Memorize it, flip the page over, and continue working.

Do not write any other hints on this page.

As you rehearse, the facts will move from your short-term memory into your long-term memory.

Answer Keys and Correcting Student Work

Use these answer keys to **provide immediate feedback.** Take a look at Ana Sample's work below.

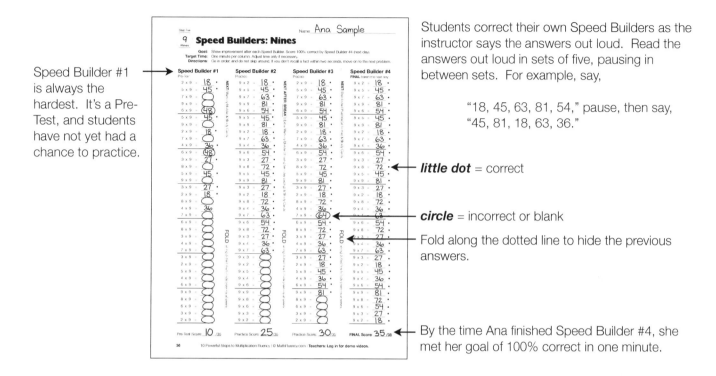

Speed Builder #1 is always the hardest. It's a Pre-Test, and students have not yet had a chance to practice.

Students correct their own Speed Builders as the instructor says the answers out loud. Read the answers out loud in sets of five, pausing in between sets. For example, say,

"18, 45, 63, 81, 54," pause, then say, "45, 81, 18, 63, 36."

little dot = correct

circle = incorrect or blank

Fold along the dotted line to hide the previous answers.

By the time Ana finished Speed Builder #4, she met her goal of 100% correct in one minute.

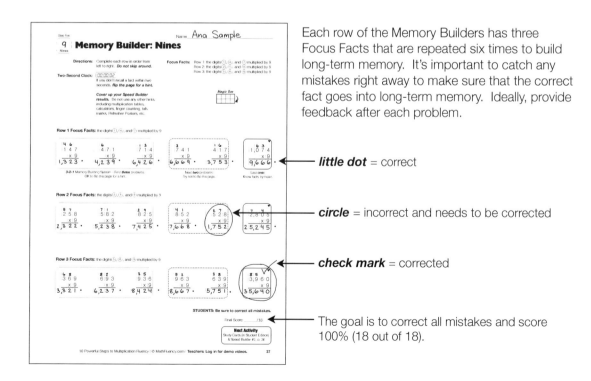

Each row of the Memory Builders has three Focus Facts that are repeated six times to build long-term memory. It's important to catch any mistakes right away to make sure that the correct fact goes into long-term memory. Ideally, provide feedback after each problem.

little dot = correct

circle = incorrect and needs to be corrected

check mark = corrected

The goal is to correct all mistakes and score 100% (18 out of 18).

2 Twos Answer Keys: Twos

Provide immediate feedback.
See page 101 for specific correction marks.

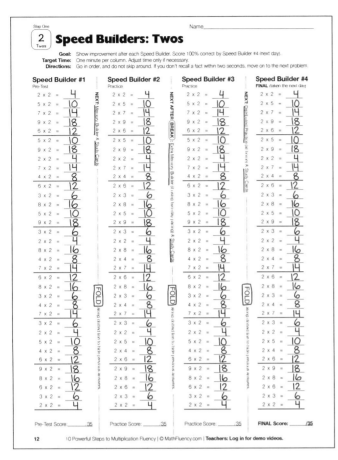

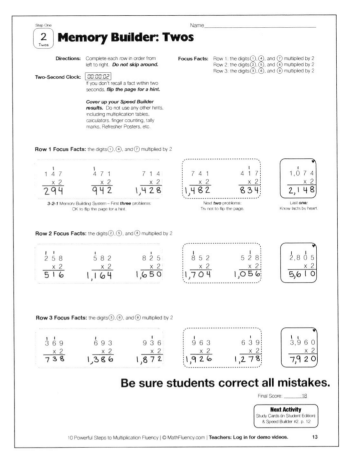

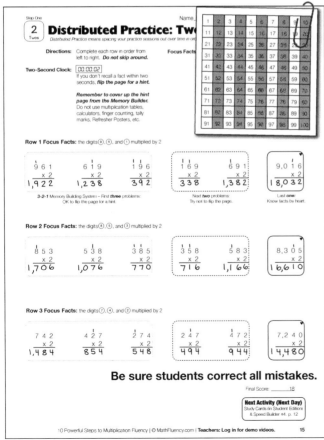

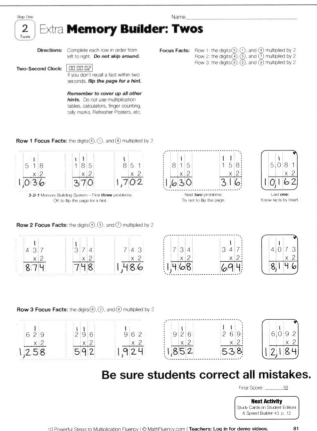

Answer Keys: Threes

Provide immediate feedback.
See page 101 for specific correction marks.

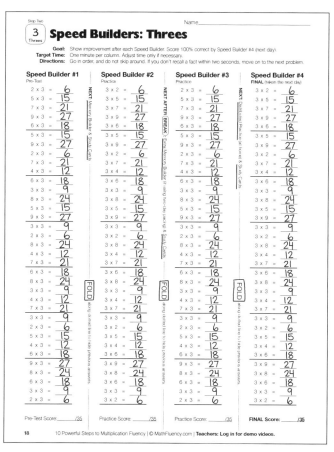

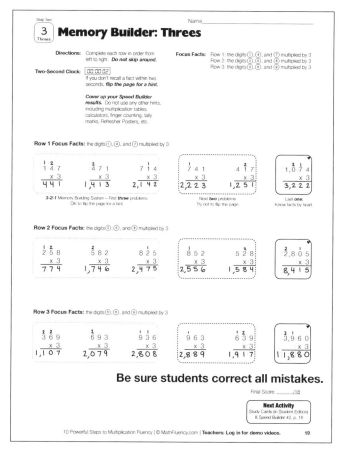

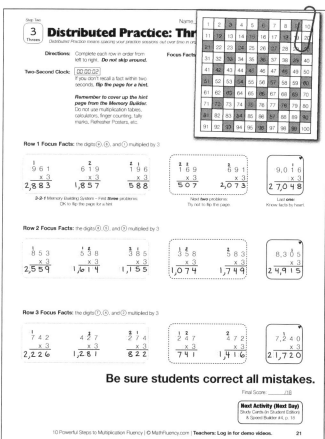

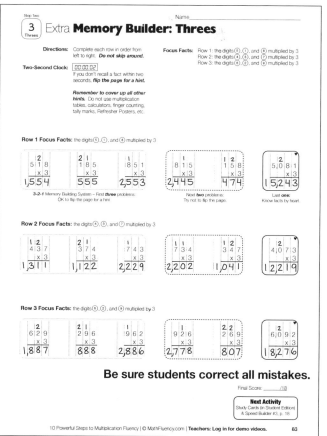

Step Three

4 Fours Answer Keys: Fours

Provide immediate feedback.
See page 101 for specific correction marks.

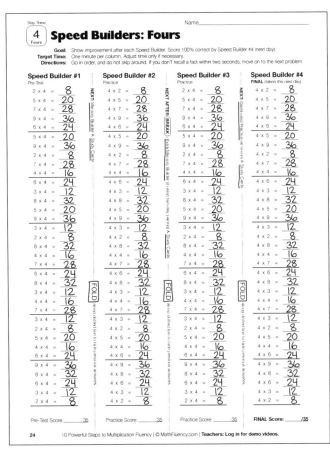

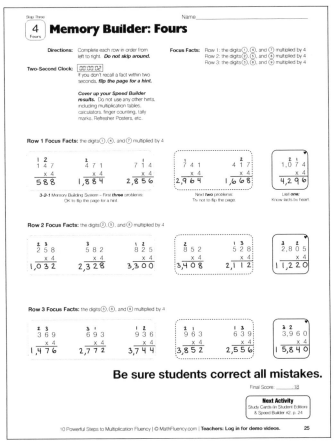

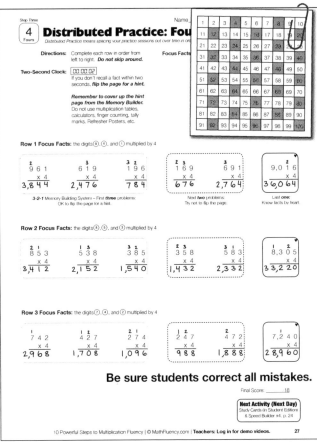

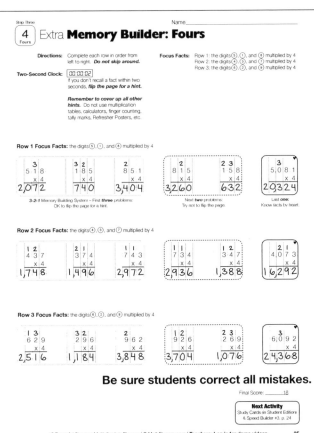

Answer Keys: Fives

Provide immediate feedback.
See page 101 for specific correction marks.

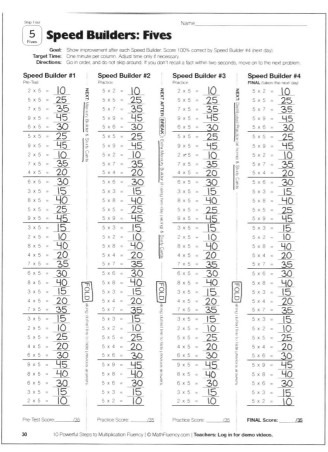

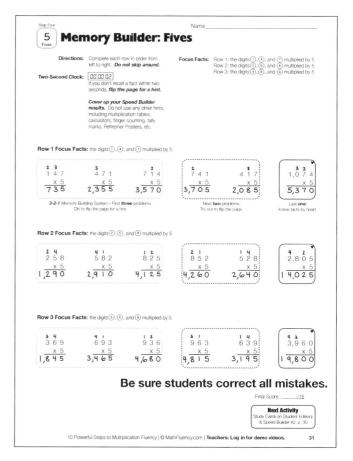

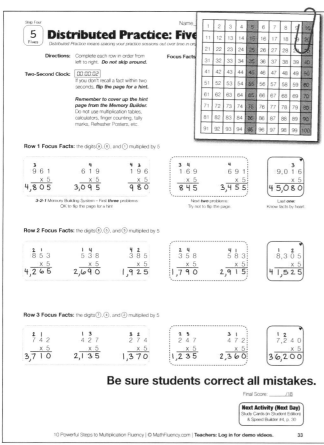

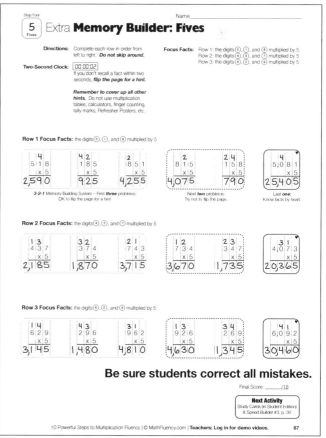

9 Nines

Answer Keys: Nines

Provide immediate feedback.
See page 101 for specific correction marks.

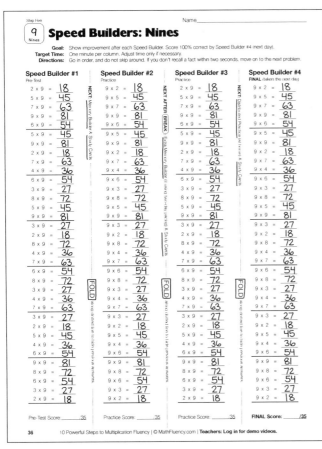

Step Five — 9 Nines — Speed Builders: Nines   Name_____

Goal: Show improvement after each Speed Builder. Score 100% correct by Speed Builder #4 (next day).
Target Time: One minute per column. Adjust time only if necessary.
Directions: Go in order, and do not skip around. If you don't recall a fact within two seconds, move on to the next problem.

Speed Builder #1 (Pre-Test):

2 x 9 =	18
5 x 9 =	45
7 x 9 =	63
9 x 9 =	81
6 x 9 =	54
5 x 9 =	45
9 x 9 =	81
2 x 9 =	18
7 x 9 =	63
4 x 9 =	36
6 x 9 =	54
3 x 9 =	27
8 x 9 =	72
5 x 9 =	45
9 x 9 =	81
3 x 9 =	27
2 x 9 =	18
8 x 9 =	72
4 x 9 =	36
7 x 9 =	63
6 x 9 =	54
8 x 9 =	72
3 x 9 =	27
4 x 9 =	36
7 x 9 =	63
3 x 9 =	27
2 x 9 =	18
5 x 9 =	45
4 x 9 =	36
6 x 9 =	54
8 x 9 =	72
6 x 9 =	54
3 x 9 =	27
2 x 9 =	18

Pre-Test Score: ___/35 Practice Score: ___/35 Practice Score: ___/35 FINAL Score: ___/35

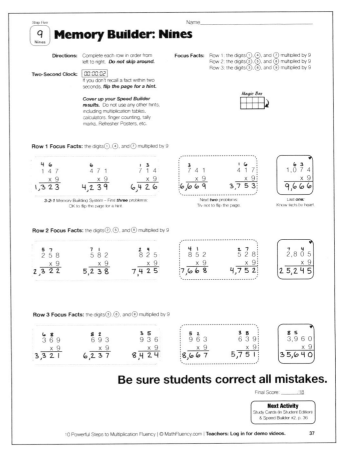

Step Five — 9 Nines — Memory Builder: Nines   Name_____

Directions: Complete each row in order from left to right. *Do not skip around.*

Focus Facts: Row 1: the digits 1, 4, and 7 multiplied by 9
Row 2: the digits 2, 5, and 8 multiplied by 9
Row 3: the digits 3, 6, and 9 multiplied by 9

Two-Second Clock: 00:00:02
If you don't recall a fact within two seconds, *flip the page for a hint.*

Cover up your Speed Builder results. Do not use any other hints, including multiplication tables, calculators, finger counting, tally marks, Refresher Posters, etc.

Magic Box

Row 1 Focus Facts: the digits 1, 4, and 7 multiplied by 9

Row 2 Focus Facts: the digits 2, 5, and 8 multiplied by 9

Row 3 Focus Facts: the digits 3, 6, and 9 multiplied by 9

Be sure students correct all mistakes.

Final Score: ___/18

Next Activity
Study Cards (in Student Edition) & Speed Builder #2, p. 36

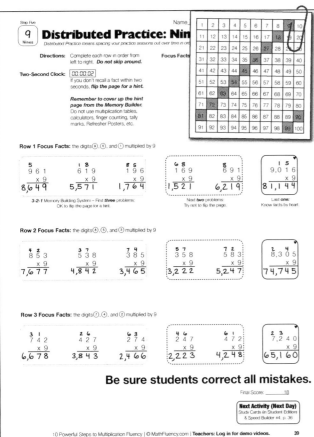

Step Five — 9 Nines — Distributed Practice: Nines   Name_____
Distributed Practice means spacing your practice sessions out over time in order...

Directions: Complete each row in order from left to right. *Do not skip around.*

Focus Facts

Two-Second Clock: 00:00:02
If you don't recall a fact within two seconds, *flip the page for a hint.*

Remember to cover up the hint page from the Memory Builder. Do not use multiplication tables, calculators, finger counting, tally marks, Refresher Posters, etc.

Row 1 Focus Facts: the digits 9, 6, and 1 multiplied by 9

Row 2 Focus Facts: the digits 8, 5, and 3 multiplied by 9

Row 3 Focus Facts: the digits 7, 4, and 2 multiplied by 9

Be sure students correct all mistakes.

Final Score: ___/18

Next Activity (Next Day)
Study Cards (in Student Edition) & Speed Builder #4, p. 36

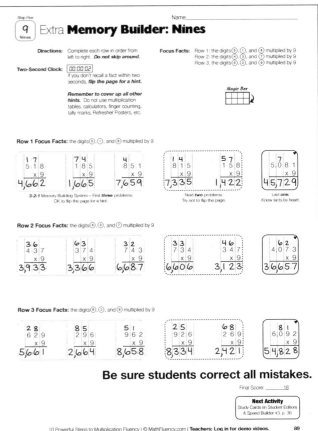

Step Five — 9 Nines — Extra Memory Builder: Nines   Name_____

Directions: Complete each row in order from left to right. *Do not skip around.*

Focus Facts: Row 1: the digits 5, 1, and 8 multiplied by 9
Row 2: the digits 4, 3, and 7 multiplied by 9
Row 3: the digits 6, 2, and 9 multiplied by 9

Two-Second Clock: 00:00:02
If you don't recall a fact within two seconds, *flip the page for a hint.*

Remember to cover up all other hints. Do not use multiplication tables, calculators, finger counting, tally marks, Refresher Posters, etc.

Magic Box

Row 1 Focus Facts: the digits 5, 1, and 8 multiplied by 9

Row 2 Focus Facts: the digits 4, 3, and 7 multiplied by 9

Row 3 Focus Facts: the digits 6, 2, and 9 multiplied by 9

Be sure students correct all mistakes.

Final Score: ___/18

Next Activity
Study Cards (in Student Edition) & Speed Builder #3, p. 36

Squares

Answer Keys: Squares

Provide immediate feedback.
See page 101 for specific correction marks.

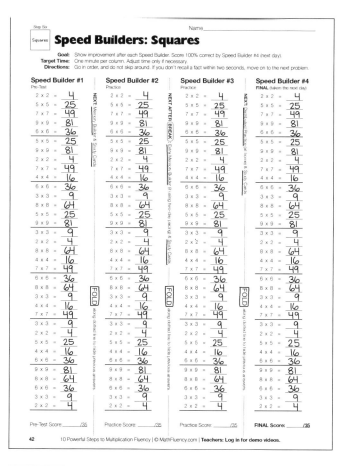

Speed Builders: Squares

Goal: Show improvement after each Speed Builder. Score 100% correct by Speed Builder #4 (next day).
Target Time: One minute per column. Adjust time only if necessary.
Directions: Go in order, and do not skip around. If you don't recall a fact within two seconds, move on to the next problem.

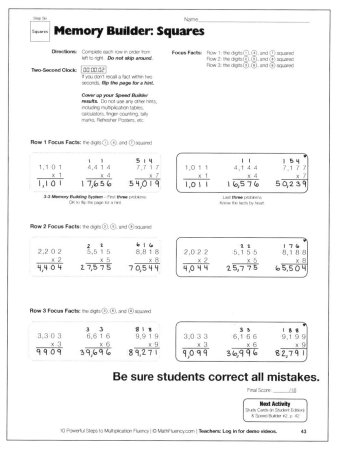

Memory Builder: Squares

Directions: Complete each row in order from left to right. **Do not skip around.**

Two-Second Clock: `00:00:02`
If you don't recall a fact within two seconds, **flip the page for a hint.**

Cover up your Speed Builder results. Do not use any other hints, including multiplication tables, calculators, finger counting, tally marks, Refresher Posters, etc.

Focus Facts: Row 1: the digits ①, ④, and ⑦ squared
Row 2: the digits ②, ⑤, and ⑧ squared
Row 3: the digits ③, ⑥, and ⑨ squared

Be sure students correct all mistakes.

Final Score: _____ /18

Next Activity
Study Cards (in Student Edition) & Speed Builder #2, p. 42

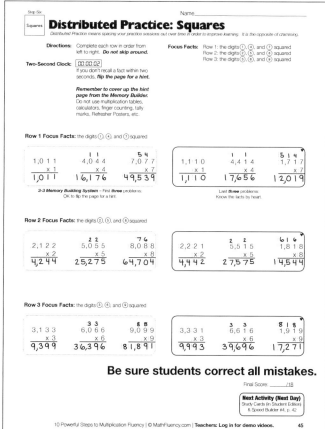

Distributed Practice: Squares

Distributed Practice means spacing your practice sessions out over time in order to improve learning. It is the opposite of cramming.

Directions: Complete each row in order from left to right. **Do not skip around.**

Two-Second Clock: `00:00:02`
If you don't recall a fact within two seconds, **flip the page for a hint.**

Remember to cover up the hint page from the Memory Builder. Do not use multiplication tables, calculators, finger counting, tally marks, Refresher Posters, etc.

Focus Facts: Row 1: the digits ①, ④, and ⑦ squared
Row 2: the digits ②, ⑤, and ⑧ squared
Row 3: the digits ③, ⑥, and ⑨ squared

Be sure students correct all mistakes.

Final Score: _____ /18

Next Activity (Next Day)
Study Cards (in Student Edition) & Speed Builder #4, p. 42

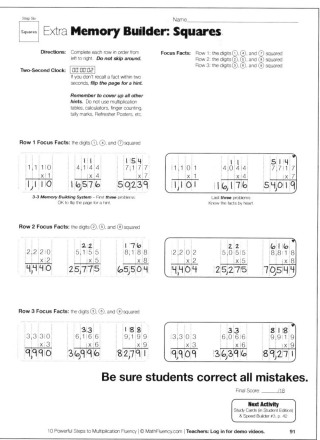

Extra Memory Builder: Squares

Directions: Complete each row in order from left to right. **Do not skip around.**

Two-Second Clock: `00:00:02`
If you don't recall a fact within two seconds, **flip the page for a hint.**

Remember to cover up all other hints. Do not use multiplication tables, calculators, finger counting, tally marks, Refresher Posters, etc.

Focus Facts: Row 1: the digits ①, ④, and ⑦ squared
Row 2: the digits ②, ⑤, and ⑧ squared
Row 3: the digits ③, ⑥, and ⑨ squared

Be sure students correct all mistakes.

Final Score: _____ /18

Next Activity
Study Cards (in Student Edition) & Speed Builder #3, p. 42

Answer Keys: Big Bad Numbers

Provide immediate feedback. See page 101 for specific correction marks.

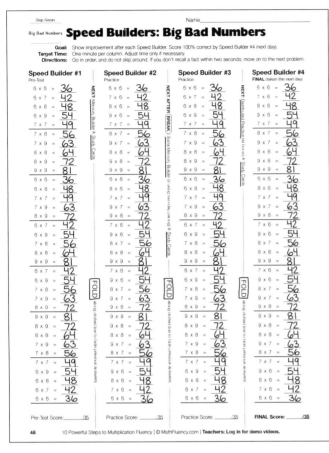

Speed Builders: Big Bad Numbers

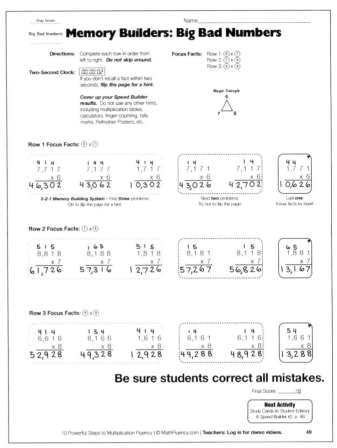

Memory Builders: Big Bad Numbers

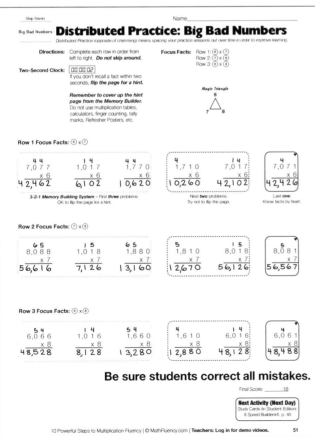

Distributed Practice: Big Bad Numbers

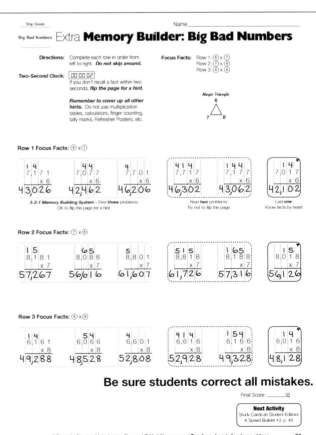

Extra Memory Builder: Big Bad Numbers

Step Eight

6 Sixes

Answer Keys: Sixes

Provide immediate feedback.
See page 101 for specific correction marks.

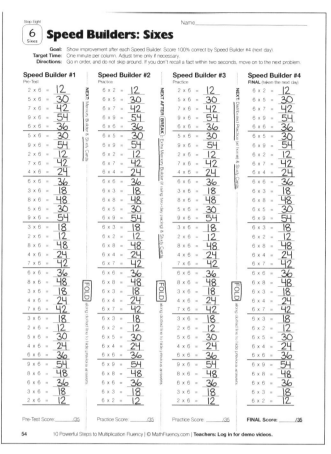

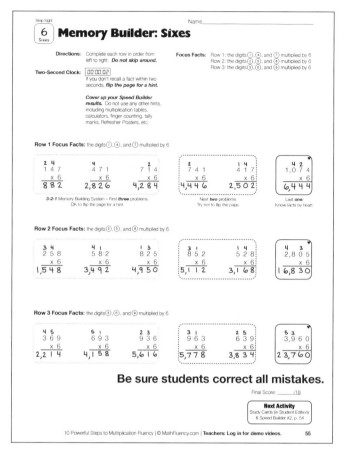

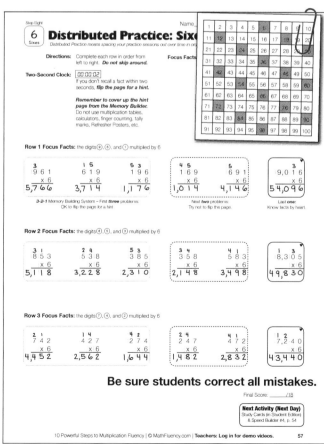

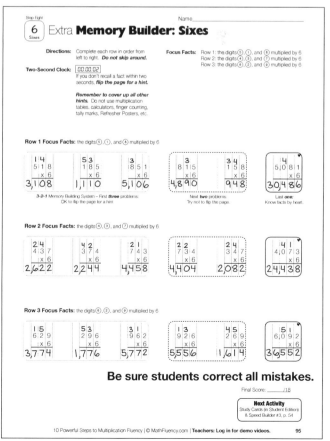

7 Sevens | Answer Keys: Sevens

Provide immediate feedback.
See page 101 for specific correction marks.

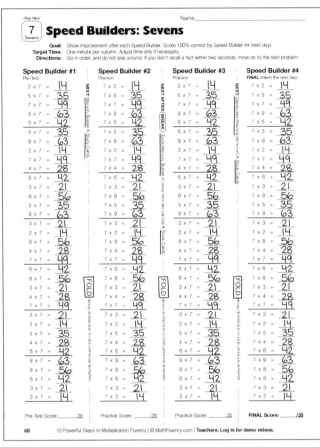

7 Sevens — Speed Builders: Sevens

Goal: Show improvement after each Speed Builder. Score 100% correct by Speed Builder #4 (next day).
Target Time: One minute per column. Adjust time only if necessary.
Directions: Go in order, and do not skip around. If you don't recall a fact within two seconds, move on to the next problem.

Speed Builder #1 — Pre-Test
Speed Builder #2 — Practice
Speed Builder #3 — Practice
Speed Builder #4 — FINAL (taken the next day)

Pre-Test Score: ___/35   Practice Score: ___/35   Practice Score: ___/35   FINAL Score: ___/35

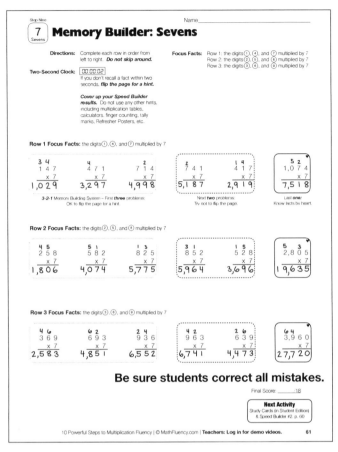

7 Sevens — Memory Builder: Sevens

Directions: Complete each row in order from left to right. *Do not skip around.*

Focus Facts: Row 1: the digits 1, 4, and 7 multiplied by 7
Row 2: the digits 2, 5, and 8 multiplied by 7
Row 3: the digits 3, 6, and 9 multiplied by 7

Two-Second Clock: 00:00:02
If you don't recall a fact within two seconds, *flip the page for a hint.*

Cover up your Speed Builder results. Do not use any other hints, including multiplication tables, calculators, finger counting, tally marks, Refresher Posters, etc.

Be sure students correct all mistakes.

Final Score: ___/18

Next Activity
Study Cards (in Student Edition)
& Speed Builder #2, p. 60

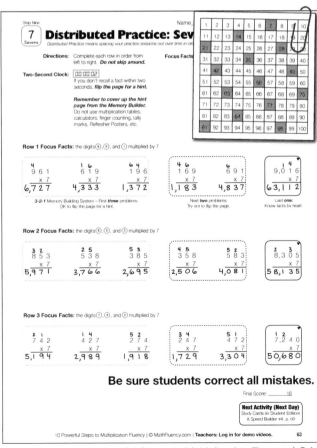

7 Sevens — Distributed Practice: Sevens

Distributed Practice means spacing your practice sessions out over time.

Directions: Complete each row in order from left to right. *Do not skip around.*

Two-Second Clock: 00:00:02
If you don't recall a fact within two seconds, *flip the page for a hint.*

Remember to cover up the hint page from the Memory Builder. Do not use multiplication tables, calculators, finger counting, tally marks, Refresher Posters, etc.

Row 1 Focus Facts: the digits 9, 6, and 1 multiplied by 7
Row 2 Focus Facts: the digits 8, 5, and 3 multiplied by 7
Row 3 Focus Facts: the digits 7, 4, and 2 multiplied by 7

Be sure students correct all mistakes.

Final Score: ___/18

Next Activity (Next Day)
Study Cards (in Student Edition)
& Speed Builder #4, p. 60

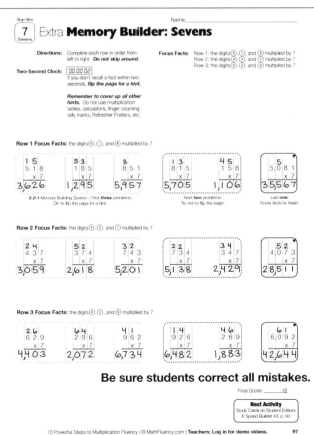

7 Sevens — Extra Memory Builder: Sevens

Directions: Complete each row in order from left to right. *Do not skip around.*

Focus Facts: Row 1: the digits 5, 1, and 8 multiplied by 7
Row 2: the digits 4, 3, and 7 multiplied by 7
Row 3: the digits 6, 2, and 9 multiplied by 7

Two-Second Clock: 00:00:02
If you don't recall a fact within two seconds, *flip the page for a hint.*

Remember to cover up all other hints. Do not use multiplication tables, calculators, finger counting, tally marks, Refresher Posters, etc.

Row 1 Focus Facts: the digits 5, 1, and 8 multiplied by 7
Row 2 Focus Facts: the digits 4, 3, and 7 multiplied by 7
Row 3 Focus Facts: the digits 6, 2, and 9 multiplied by 7

Be sure students correct all mistakes.

Final Score: ___/18

Next Activity
Study Cards (in Student Edition)
& Speed Builder #3, p. 60

8 Eights — Answer Keys: Eights

Provide immediate feedback.
See page 101 for specific correction marks.

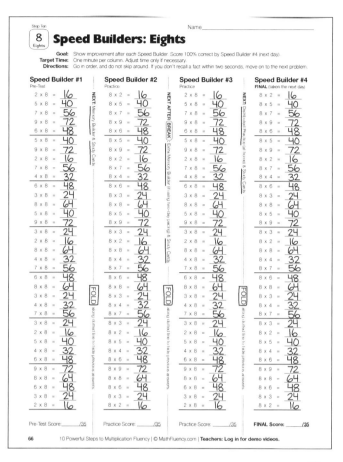

Speed Builders: Eights

Goal: Show improvement after each Speed Builder. Score 100% correct by Speed Builder #4 (next day).
Target Time: One minute per column. Adjust time only if necessary.
Directions: Go in order, and do not skip around. If you don't recall a fact within two seconds, move on to the next problem.

Speed Builder #1 (Pre-Test)

2 x 8 =	16
5 x 8 =	40
7 x 8 =	56
9 x 8 =	72
6 x 8 =	48
5 x 8 =	40
9 x 8 =	72
2 x 8 =	16
7 x 8 =	56
4 x 8 =	32
6 x 8 =	48
3 x 8 =	24
5 x 8 =	40
9 x 8 =	72
3 x 8 =	24
2 x 8 =	16
8 x 8 =	64
4 x 8 =	32
7 x 8 =	56
6 x 8 =	48
8 x 8 =	64
3 x 8 =	24
4 x 8 =	32
7 x 8 =	56
3 x 8 =	24
2 x 8 =	16
5 x 8 =	40
4 x 8 =	32
6 x 8 =	48
9 x 8 =	72
8 x 8 =	64
3 x 8 =	24
2 x 8 =	16

Pre-Test Score: ____/35

Speed Builder #2 (Practice)

8 x 2 =	40
8 x 7 =	56
8 x 6 =	48
8 x 5 =	40
8 x 9 =	72
8 x 2 =	16
8 x 7 =	56
8 x 4 =	32
8 x 6 =	48
8 x 3 =	24
8 x 8 =	64
8 x 5 =	40
8 x 9 =	72
8 x 3 =	24
8 x 2 =	16
8 x 8 =	64
8 x 4 =	32
8 x 7 =	56
8 x 6 =	48
8 x 3 =	24
8 x 4 =	32
8 x 7 =	56
8 x 3 =	24
8 x 2 =	16
8 x 5 =	40
8 x 4 =	32
8 x 9 =	72
8 x 8 =	64
8 x 6 =	48
8 x 3 =	24
8 x 2 =	16

Practice Score: ____/35

Speed Builder #3 (Practice)

2 x 8 =	16
5 x 8 =	40
7 x 8 =	56
9 x 8 =	72
6 x 8 =	48
5 x 8 =	40
9 x 8 =	72
2 x 8 =	16
7 x 8 =	56
4 x 8 =	32
6 x 8 =	48
3 x 8 =	24
8 x 8 =	64
5 x 8 =	40
8 x 9 =	72
3 x 8 =	24
2 x 8 =	16
8 x 8 =	64
4 x 8 =	32
7 x 8 =	56
6 x 8 =	48
8 x 8 =	64
3 x 8 =	24
8 x 4 =	32
7 x 8 =	56
3 x 8 =	24
2 x 8 =	16
5 x 8 =	40
4 x 8 =	32
6 x 8 =	48
9 x 8 =	72
8 x 8 =	64
8 x 6 =	48
3 x 8 =	24
2 x 8 =	16

Practice Score: ____/35

Speed Builder #4 (FINAL, taken the next day)

8 x 2 =	16
8 x 5 =	40
8 x 7 =	56
8 x 6 =	48
8 x 5 =	40
8 x 2 =	16
8 x 7 =	56
8 x 6 =	48
8 x 5 =	40
8 x 9 =	72
8 x 2 =	16
8 x 7 =	56
8 x 6 =	48
8 x 3 =	24
8 x 4 =	32
8 x 7 =	56
8 x 3 =	24
8 x 4 =	32
8 x 7 =	56
8 x 3 =	24
8 x 2 =	16
8 x 5 =	40
8 x 4 =	32
8 x 6 =	48
8 x 9 =	72
8 x 8 =	64
8 x 6 =	48
8 x 3 =	24
8 x 2 =	16

FINAL Score: ____/35

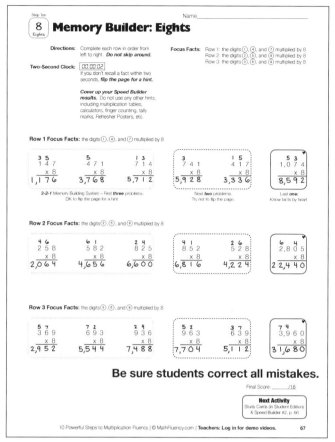

8 Eights — Memory Builder: Eights

Directions: Complete each row in order from left to right. *Do not skip around.*

Focus Facts: Row 1: the digits 1, 4, and 7 multiplied by 8
Row 2: the digits 2, 5, and 8 multiplied by 8
Row 3: the digits 3, 6, and 9 multiplied by 8

Two-Second Clock: 00:00:02
If you don't recall a fact within two seconds, **flip the page for a hint.**

Cover up your Speed Builder results. Do not use any other hints, including multiplication tables, calculators, finger counting, tally marks, Refresher Posters, etc.

Row 1 Focus Facts: the digits 1, 4, and 7 multiplied by 8

| 35 / 147 x8 = 1,176 | 5 / 471 x8 = 3,768 | 13 / 714 x8 = 5,712 | 3 / 741 x8 = 5,928 | 15 / 417 x8 = 3,336 | 53 / 1,074 x8 = 8,592 |

3-2-1 Memory Building System – First *three* problems. OK to flip the page for a hint.
Next *two* problems. Try not to flip the page.
Last *one:* Know facts by heart

Row 2 Focus Facts: the digits 2, 5, and 8 multiplied by 8

| 46 / 258 x8 = 2,064 | 61 / 582 x8 = 4,656 | 24 / 825 x8 = 6,600 | 41 / 852 x8 = 6,816 | 26 / 528 x8 = 4,224 | 64 / 2,805 x8 = 22,440 |

Row 3 Focus Facts: the digits 3, 6, and 9 multiplied by 8

| 57 / 369 x8 = 2,952 | 72 / 693 x8 = 5,544 | 24 / 936 x8 = 7,488 | 52 / 963 x8 = 7,704 | 37 / 639 x8 = 5,112 | 74 / 3,960 x8 = 31,680 |

Be sure students correct all mistakes.

Final Score: ____/18

Next Activity
Study Cards (in Student Edition)
& Speed Builder #2, p. 66

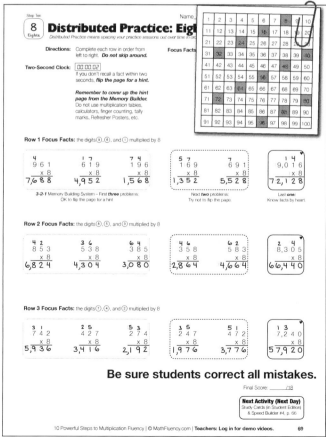

8 Eights — Distributed Practice: Eights

Distributed Practice means spacing your practice sessions out over time in order...

Directions: Complete each row in order from left to right. *Do not skip around.*

Two-Second Clock: 00:00:02
If you don't recall a fact within two seconds, **flip the page for a hint.**

Remember to cover up the hint page from the Memory Builder. Do not use multiplication tables, calculators, finger counting, tally marks, Refresher Posters, etc.

Row 1 Focus Facts: the digits 9, 6, and 1 multiplied by 8

| 4 / 961 x8 = 7,688 | 17 / 619 x8 = 4,952 | 74 / 196 x8 = 1,568 | 57 / 169 x8 = 1,352 | 7 / 691 x8 = 5,528 | 14 / 9,016 x8 = 72,128 |

3-2-1 Memory Building System – First *three* problems. OK to flip the page for a hint
Next *two* problems. Try not to flip the page.
Last *one:* Know facts by heart

Row 2 Focus Facts: the digits 8, 5, and 3 multiplied by 8

| 42 / 853 x8 = 6,824 | 36 / 538 x8 = 4,304 | 64 / 385 x8 = 3,080 | 46 / 358 x8 = 2,864 | 62 / 583 x8 = 4,664 | 24 / 8,305 x8 = 66,440 |

Row 3 Focus Facts: the digits 7, 4, and 2 multiplied by 8

| 31 / 742 x8 = 5,936 | 25 / 427 x8 = 3,416 | 53 / 274 x8 = 2,192 | 35 / 247 x8 = 1,976 | 51 / 472 x8 = 3,776 | 13 / 7,240 x8 = 57,920 |

Be sure students correct all mistakes.

Final Score: ____/18

Next Activity (Next Day)
Study Cards (in Student Edition)
& Speed Builder #4, p. 66

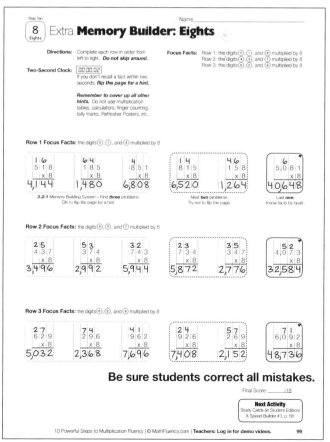

8 Eights — Extra Memory Builder: Eights

Directions: Complete each row in order from left to right. *Do not skip around.*

Focus Facts: Row 1: the digits 5, 1, and 8 multiplied by 8
Row 2: the digits 4, 3, and 7 multiplied by 8
Row 3: the digits 6, 2, and 9 multiplied by 8

Two-Second Clock: 00:00:02
If you don't recall a fact within two seconds, **flip the page for a hint.**

Remember to cover up all other hints. Do not use multiplication tables, calculators, finger counting, tally marks, Refresher Posters, etc.

Row 1 Focus Facts: the digits 5, 1, and 8 multiplied by 8

| 16 / 518 x8 = 4,144 | 64 / 185 x8 = 1,480 | 4 / 851 x8 = 6,808 | 14 / 815 x8 = 6,520 | 46 / 158 x8 = 1,264 | 16 / 5,081 x8 = 40,648 |

3-2-1 Memory Building System – First *three* problems. OK to flip the page for a hint
Next *two* problems. Try not to flip the page.
Last *one:* Know facts by heart

Row 2 Focus Facts: the digits 4, 3, and 7 multiplied by 8

| 25 / 437 x8 = 3,496 | 53 / 374 x8 = 2,992 | 32 / 743 x8 = 5,944 | 23 / 734 x8 = 5,872 | 35 / 347 x8 = 2,776 | 52 / 4,073 x8 = 32,584 |

Row 3 Focus Facts: the digits 6, 2, and 9 multiplied by 8

| 27 / 629 x8 = 5,032 | 74 / 296 x8 = 2,368 | 41 / 962 x8 = 7,696 | 24 / 926 x8 = 7,408 | 57 / 269 x8 = 2,152 | 71 / 6,092 x8 = 48,736 |

Be sure students correct all mistakes.

Final Score: ____/18

Next Activity
Study Cards (in Student Edition)
& Speed Builder #3, p. 66

Answer Keys: Appendix A

Use Appendix A as guided lessons **_BEFORE_** starting Step One (The Twos).

Appendix A-1: Multiplication is a Shortcut for Repeated Addition

Directions: Diagram each problem, and show how multiplication is just a short way of describing repeated addition.

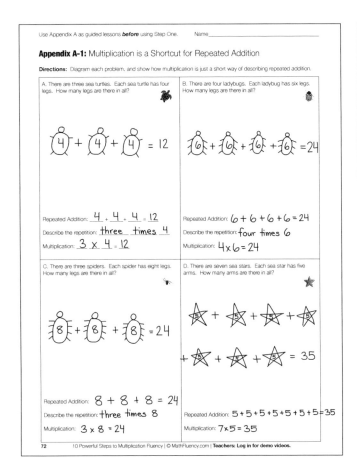

A. There are three sea turtles. Each sea turtle has four legs. How many legs are there in all?

Repeated Addition: $4 + 4 + 4 = 12$

Describe the repetition: three times 4

Multiplication: $3 \times 4 = 12$

B. There are four ladybugs. Each ladybug has six legs. How many legs are there in all?

Repeated Addition: $6 + 6 + 6 + 6 = 24$

Describe the repetition: four times 6

Multiplication: $4 \times 6 = 24$

C. There are three spiders. Each spider has eight legs. How many legs are there in all?

Repeated Addition: $8 + 8 + 8 = 24$

Describe the repetition: three times 8

Multiplication: $3 \times 8 = 24$

D. There are seven sea stars. Each sea star has five arms. How many arms are there in all?

Repeated Addition: $5 + 5 + 5 + 5 + 5 + 5 + 5 = 35$

Multiplication: $7 \times 5 = 35$

Appendix A-2: Repeated Addition Using Arrays

Part 1: An array is an ordered arrangement using rows and columns. Show each array as a repeated addition problem and as a multiplication problem. (Note: It's conventional to list rows first, then columns. For example, a 2 x 5 array has 2 rows and 5 columns, and a 5 x 2 array has 5 rows and 2 columns.)

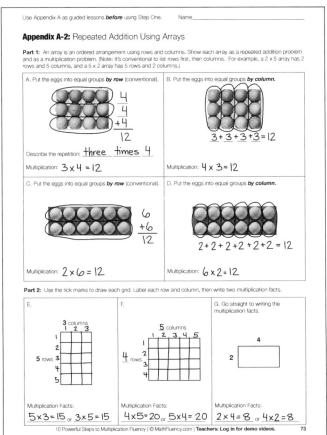

A. Put the eggs into equal groups **by row** (conventional).

$\frac{\begin{array}{r}4\\4\\+4\end{array}}{12}$

Describe the repetition: three times 4

Multiplication: $3 \times 4 = 12$

B. Put the eggs into equal groups **by column**.

$3 + 3 + 3 + 3 = 12$

Multiplication: $4 \times 3 = 12$

C. Put the eggs into equal groups **by row** (conventional).

$\frac{\begin{array}{r}6\\+6\end{array}}{12}$

Multiplication: $2 \times 6 = 12$

D. Put the eggs into equal groups **by column**.

$2 + 2 + 2 + 2 + 2 + 2 = 12$

Multiplication: $6 \times 2 = 12$

Part 2: Use the tick marks to draw each grid. Label each row and column, then write two multiplication facts.

E. 3 columns, 5 rows

Multiplication Facts: $5 \times 3 = 15$ or $3 \times 5 = 15$

F. 5 columns, 4 rows

Multiplication Facts: $4 \times 5 = 20$ or $5 \times 4 = 20$

G. Go straight to writing the multiplication facts. (4, 2)

Multiplication Facts: $2 \times 4 = 8$ or $4 \times 2 = 8$

Appendix A-3: Repeated Addition Using Number Lines

Directions: Label each number line to show how repeated addition is the same as multiplication.

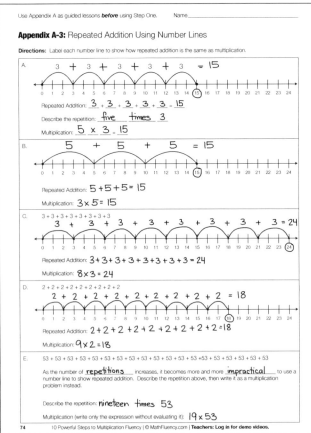

A. $3 + 3 + 3 + 3 + 3 = 15$

Repeated Addition: $3 + 3 + 3 + 3 + 3 = 15$

Describe the repetition: five times 3

Multiplication: $5 \times 3 = 15$

B. $5 + 5 + 5 = 15$

Repeated Addition: $5 + 5 + 5 = 15$

Multiplication: $3 \times 5 = 15$

C. $3 + 3 + 3 + 3 + 3 + 3 + 3 + 3 = 24$

Repeated Addition: $3 + 3 + 3 + 3 + 3 + 3 + 3 + 3 = 24$

Multiplication: $8 \times 3 = 24$

D. $2 + 2 + 2 + 2 + 2 + 2 + 2 + 2 + 2 = 18$

Repeated Addition: $2 + 2 + 2 + 2 + 2 + 2 + 2 + 2 + 2 = 18$

Multiplication: $9 \times 2 = 18$

E. $53 + 53 + 53 + 53 + 53 + 53 + 53 + 53 + 53 + 53 + 53 + 53 + 53 + 53 + 53 + 53 + 53 + 53 + 53$

As the number of __repetitions__ increases, it becomes more and more __impractical__ to use a number line to show repeated addition. Describe the repetition above, then write it as a multiplication problem instead.

Describe the repetition: nineteen times 53

Multiplication (write only the expression without evaluating it): 19×53

Appendix A-4: Repeated Addition Using Skip Counting on a Hundred Chart

Part 1: Use the Hundred Charts to skip count. Lightly shade in the correct boxes to reveal a hidden pattern.

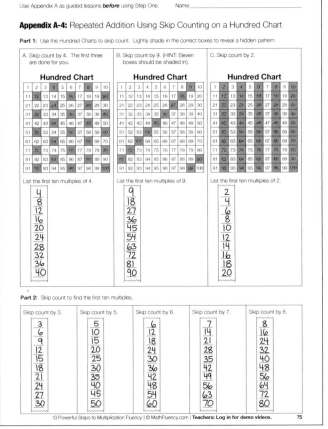

A. Skip count by 4. The first three are done for you.

List the first ten multiples of 4.
4, 8, 12, 16, 20, 24, 28, 32, 36, 40

B. Skip count by 9. (HINT: Eleven boxes should be shaded in.)

List the first ten multiples of 9.
9, 18, 27, 36, 45, 54, 63, 72, 81, 90

C. Skip count by 2.

List the first ten multiples of 2.
2, 4, 6, 8, 10, 12, 14, 16, 18, 20

Part 2: Skip count to find the first ten multiples.

Skip count by 3.	Skip count by 5.	Skip count by 6.	Skip count by 7.	Skip count by 8.
3	5	6	7	8
6	10	12	14	16
9	15	18	21	24
12	20	24	28	32
15	25	30	35	40
18	30	36	42	48
21	35	42	49	56
24	40	48	56	64
27	45	54	63	72
30	50	60	70	80

Answer Keys: Appendix B

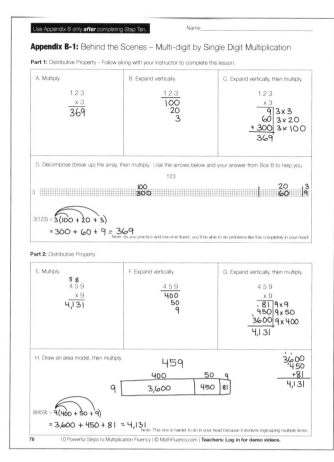

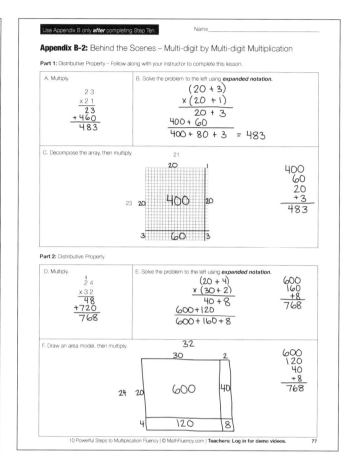

Appendix B-1, B-2, and B-3

Please remember that Appendix B should be used only **AFTER** all ten steps of the Magic Sequence have completed.

During Steps 1-10, the Memory Builders and Distributed Practice are designed to use multi-digit multiplication and the **standard algorithm** to help students memorize their single-digit facts (see the demo videos).

Then, once students have memorized all of their basic facts, Appendix B gives a behind-the scenes look at multi-digit multiplication, including using expanded notation, the distributive property, and area models.

In **Appendix B-3,** students will practice multiplying multi-digit by single-digit numbers in their head. This requires them to have their single-digit facts memorized, and it involves multiplying and adding from left to right (instead of from right to left) using expanded notation.

Notice how Box A1 helps students with Box C. Think of "420 + 18" as "420 + 10 + 8," which you can easily add in your head going from left to right. To add 420 + 10 + 8, just keep a running tally in your mind as you add from left to right and think, "420... 430... 438."

Appendix B-3: Multiplying Multi-digit by Single-digit Numbers in Your Head

Part 1: Add. You should be able to do these problems in your head (add the tens, then add the ones).

A1.	A2.	B1.	B2.
420 + 10 + 8 = **438**	120 + 16 = **136**	350 + 20 + 1 = **371**	360 + 24 = **384**
560 + 10 + 4 = **574**	360 + 12 = **372**	360 + 20 + 4 = **384**	560 + 28 = **588**
120 + 10 + 6 = **136**	420 + 18 = **438**	560 + 20 + 8 = **588**	630 + 27 = **657**
360 + 10 + 2 = **372**	560 + 14 = **574**	630 + 20 + 7 = **657**	350 + 21 = **371**

Part 2: Follow along with your instructor to multiply from **LEFT to RIGHT** using *expanded notation*.

C. (Use Box A1. to help you.)
7 | 3
× 6
420 Step i. 70 × 6
+ 18 Step ii. 3 × 6
438 Step iii. Add.

D.
8 | 2
× 7
560 Step i. 80 × 7
+ 14 Step ii. 2 × 7
574 Step iii. Add.

E. (Use Box B1. to help you.)
5 | 3
× 7
350 Step i. 50 × 7
+ 21 Step ii. 3 × 7
371 Step iii. Add.

F.
9 | 6
× 4
360 Step i. 90 × 4
+ 24 Step ii. 6 × 4
384 Step iii. Add.

Part 3: Multiply in your head going from **LEFT to RIGHT.** Mentally use the same steps as in Parts 1 and 2.

G. 3 | 4 × 4 = **136**
H. 6 | 2 × 6 = **372**
I. 7 | 3 × 9 = **657**
J. 8 | 4 × 7 = **588**

Part 4: Add. You should be able to do these problems in your head.

K1.	K2.
200 + 60 + 10 + 2 = **272**	600 + 210 + 12 = **822**
600 + 200 + 10 + 10 + 2 = **822**	1,200 + 60 + 9 = **1,269**
800 + 100 + 60 + 10 + 2 = **972**	200 + 60 + 12 = **272**
1,000 + 200 + 60 + 9 = **1,269**	800 + 160 + 12 = **972**

Part 5: Follow along with your instructor to multiply from **LEFT to RIGHT** using *expanded notation*. Use Part 4 to help you. With plenty of practice, you will be able to do these types of problems completely in your head.

L. (Use Box K1. to help you.)
1 | 3 | 6
× 2
200 Step i. 100 × 2
60 Step ii. 30 × 2
+ 12 Step iii. 6 × 2
272 Step iv. Add.

M.
4 | 2 | 3
× 3
1,200 Step i. 400 × 3
60 Step ii. 20 × 3
+ 9 Step iii. 3 × 3
1,269 Step iv. Add.

N.
2 | 7 | 4
× 3
600 Step i. 200 × 3
210 Step ii. 70 × 3
+ 12 Step iii. 4 × 3
822 Step iv. Add.

O.
4 | 8 | 6
× 2
800 Step i. 400 × 2
160 Step ii. 80 × 2
+ 12 Step iii. 6 × 2
972 Step iv. Add.

Name _____ Date _____ Percent Correct (100 problems) _____

Single-digit Multiplication Pretest and Posttest

Directions: Students have **four minutes** to complete this single-digit multiplication assessment. If students cannot recall a fact within two seconds, they should skip the problem and move on to the next one that they do know.

7	1	5	2	6	9	3	8	0	4
x1	x1	x1	x1	x1	x1	x1	x1	x1	x1

7	1	5	2	6	9	3	8	0	4
x0	x0	x0	x0	x0	x0	x0	x0	x0	x0

7	1	5	2	6	9	3	8	0	4
x9	x9	x9	x9	x9	x9	x9	x9	x9	x9

7	1	5	2	6	9	3	8	0	4
x4	x4	x4	x4	x4	x4	x4	x4	x4	x4

7	1	5	2	6	9	3	8	0	4
x7	x7	x7	x7	x7	x7	x7	x7	x7	x7

7	1	5	2	6	9	3	8	0	4
x8	x8	x8	x8	x8	x8	x8	x8	x8	x8

7	1	5	2	6	9	3	8	0	4
x3	x3	x3	x3	x3	x3	x3	x3	x3	x3

7	1	5	2	6	9	3	8	0	4
x6	x6	x6	x6	x6	x6	x6	x6	x6	x6

7	1	5	2	6	9	3	8	0	4
x2	x2	x2	x2	x2	x2	x2	x2	x2	x2

7	1	5	2	6	9	3	8	0	4
x5	x5	x5	x5	x5	x5	x5	x5	x5	x5

Multi-digit by Single-digit Multiplication Pretest and Posttest

Directions: Students have **seven minutes** to complete this multi-digit multiplication assessment. Students should use the standard algorithm for this set of problems.

A. $\begin{array}{r} 4\ 6\ 9 \\ \times\ 3 \\ \hline \end{array}$	B. $\begin{array}{r} 9\ 1\ 7 \\ \times\ 4 \\ \hline \end{array}$	C. $\begin{array}{r} 6\ 8\ 7 \\ \times\ 7 \\ \hline \end{array}$	D. $\begin{array}{r} 2\ 8\ 7 \\ \times\ 6 \\ \hline \end{array}$
E. $\begin{array}{r} 8\ 7\ 6 \\ \times\ 8 \\ \hline \end{array}$	F. $\begin{array}{r} 4\ 0\ 6 \\ \times\ 6 \\ \hline \end{array}$	G. $\begin{array}{r} 8\ 3\ 6 \\ \times\ 4 \\ \hline \end{array}$	H. $\begin{array}{r} 7\ 0\ 8 \\ \times\ 3 \\ \hline \end{array}$
I. $\begin{array}{r} 5\ 1\ 8 \\ \times\ 7 \\ \hline \end{array}$	J. $\begin{array}{r} 2\ 5\ 4 \\ \times\ 4 \\ \hline \end{array}$	K. $\begin{array}{r} 1\ 3\ 5 \\ \times\ 6 \\ \hline \end{array}$	L. $\begin{array}{r} 3\ 6\ 7 \\ \times\ 9 \\ \hline \end{array}$
M. $\begin{array}{r} 3\ 5\ 7 \\ \times\ 8 \\ \hline \end{array}$	N. $\begin{array}{r} 9\ 1\ 5 \\ \times\ 9 \\ \hline \end{array}$	O. $\begin{array}{r} 1\ 8\ 6 \\ \times\ 8 \\ \hline \end{array}$	P. $\begin{array}{r} 9\ 2\ 6 \\ \times\ 7 \\ \hline \end{array}$
Q. $\begin{array}{r} 4\ 0\ 8 \\ \times\ 9 \\ \hline \end{array}$	R. $\begin{array}{r} 4\ 3\ 7 \\ \times\ 7 \\ \hline \end{array}$	S. $\begin{array}{r} 2\ 7\ 6 \\ \times\ 9 \\ \hline \end{array}$	T. $\begin{array}{r} 2\ 7\ 4 \\ \times\ 8 \\ \hline \end{array}$

Pretest and Posttest Answer Keys

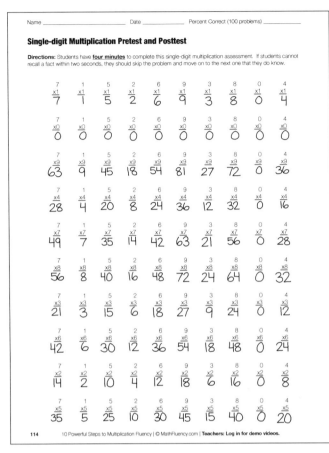

Name _____ Date _____ Percent Correct (100 problems) _____

Single-digit Multiplication Pretest and Posttest

Directions: Students have **four minutes** to complete this single-digit multiplication assessment. If students cannot recall a fact within two seconds, they should skip the problem and move on to the next one that they do know.

7 x1 7	1 x1 1	5 x1 5	2 x1 2	6 x1 6	9 x1 9	3 x1 3	8 x1 8	0 x1 0	4 x1 4
7 x0 0	1 x0 0	5 x0 0	2 x0 0	6 x0 0	9 x0 0	3 x0 0	8 x0 0	0 x0 0	4 x0 0
7 x9 63	1 x9 9	5 x9 45	2 x9 18	6 x9 54	9 x9 81	3 x9 27	8 x9 72	0 x9 0	4 x9 36
7 x4 28	1 x4 4	5 x4 20	2 x4 8	6 x4 24	9 x4 36	3 x4 12	8 x4 32	0 x4 0	4 x4 16
7 x7 49	1 x7 7	5 x7 35	2 x7 14	6 x7 42	9 x7 63	3 x7 21	8 x7 56	0 x7 0	4 x7 28
7 x8 56	1 x8 8	5 x8 40	2 x8 16	6 x8 48	9 x8 72	3 x8 24	8 x8 64	0 x8 0	4 x8 32
7 x3 21	1 x3 3	5 x3 15	2 x3 6	6 x3 18	9 x3 27	3 x3 9	8 x3 24	0 x3 0	4 x3 12
7 x6 42	1 x6 6	5 x6 30	2 x6 12	6 x6 36	9 x6 54	3 x6 18	8 x6 48	0 x6 0	4 x6 24
7 x2 14	1 x2 2	5 x2 10	2 x2 4	6 x2 12	9 x2 18	3 x2 6	8 x2 16	0 x2 0	4 x2 8
7 x5 35	1 x5 5	5 x5 25	2 x5 10	6 x5 30	9 x5 45	3 x5 15	8 x5 40	0 x5 0	4 x5 20

10 Powerful Steps to Multiplication Fluency | © MathFluency.com | **Teachers: Log in for demo videos.**

Name _____ Date _____ Percent Correct (20 problems) _____

Multi-digit by Single-digit Multiplication Pretest and Posttest

Directions: Students have **seven minutes** to complete this multi-digit multiplication assessment. Students should use the standard algorithm for this set of problems.

A. 2 2 4 6 9 x 3 **1,407**	B. 2 9 1 7 x 4 **3,668**	C. 6 4 6 8 7 x 7 **4,809**	D. 5 4 2 8 7 x 6 **1,722**
E. 6 4 8 7 6 x 8 **7,008**	F. 3 4 0 6 x 6 **2,436**	G. 1 2 8 3 6 x 4 **3,344**	H. 2 7 0 8 x 3 **2,124**
I. 1 5 5 1 8 x 7 **3,626**	J. 2 1 2 5 4 x 4 **1,016**	K. 2 3 1 3 5 x 6 **810**	L. 6 6 3 6 7 x 9 **3,303**
M. 4 5 3 5 7 x 8 **2,856**	N. 1 4 9 1 5 x 9 **8,235**	O. 6 4 1 8 6 x 8 **1,488**	P. 1 4 9 2 6 x 7 **6,482**
Q. 7 4 0 8 x 9 **3,672**	R. 2 4 4 3 7 x 7 **3,059**	S. 6 5 2 7 6 x 9 **2,484**	T. 5 3 2 7 4 x 8 **2,192**

10 Powerful Steps to Multiplication Fluency | © MathFluency.com | **Teachers: Log in for demo videos.**

Single-digit Multiplication Pretest and Posttest

Teachers may administer the single-digit multiplication *pretest* before students start using this multiplication fluency system.

Once students complete the entire multiplication fluency system, teachers may administer the same test as a *posttest.*

Students should be given four minutes to complete all 100 single-digit problems. If students cannot recall a fact within two seconds, they should skip the problem and move on to the next fact that they do know.

Multi-digit by Single-digit Multiplication Pretest and Posttest

Teachers may administer the multi-digit by single-digit multiplication *pretest* before students start using this multiplication fluency system.

Once students complete the entire multiplication fluency system, teachers may administer the same test as a *posttest.*

Students should be given seven minutes to complete all 20 multi-digit problems. Students should use the standard algorithm for this set of problems.

Made in the USA
Middletown, DE
22 March 2017